CW01514106

BAR~~DADOS~~

(Caribbean)

1993

Hayit Publishing

1st Edition 1993
UK Edition: ISBN 1 874251 02 9
US Edition: ISBN 1 56634 012 8

copyright 1993
  UK Edition: Hayit Publishing GB, Ltd, London
  US Edition: Hayit Publishing USA, Inc., New York

copyright 1991 original version: Hayit Verlag GmbH
  Cologne/Germany

Author: Helge Sobik
Translation, Adaption, Revision: Scott Reznik
Print: Scholma Druk, Bedum, NL
Photography: Helge Sobik, Barbados Board of Tourism

All rights reserved
                          Printed in the Netherlands

BARBADOS

North Point

*
Archer's Bay

ATLANTIC OCEAN

● Six Men's
Bay

● Speightstown

Turner's Hall
Woods *

▲ ● Bathsheba
Mount Hillaby
340m

* Welohman Hall Gully

● Holetown

*
Harrison's Cave

Ragged Point

■ BRIDGETOWN

Crane ●

Worthing
● St. Lawrence ●
Hastings ● Maxwell
Dover ● ● Oistins

South Point

CARIBBEAN SEA

Δ
N

0   10km

Contents

Using this Book

Books in the *Practical Travel* series offer a wealth of practical information. You will find the most important tips for your travels conveniently arranged in alphabetical order. Cross-references aid in orientation so that even entries which are not covered in depth, for instance ''Holiday Apartments,'' lead you to the appropriate entry, in this case ''Accommodation.'' Also thematically altered entries are also cross-referenced. For example under the heading ''Medication,'' there appear the following references: ''Medical Care,'' ''Pharmacies,'' ''Vaccinations.'' With travel guides from the *Practical Travel* series the information is already available before you depart on your trip. Thus, you are already familiar with necessary travel documents and maps, even customs regulations. Travel within the country is made easier through comprehensive presentation of public transportation, car rentals in addition to the practical tips ranging from medical assistance to newspapers available in the country. The descriptions of cities are arranged alphabetically as well and include the most important facts about the particular city, its history and a summary of significant sights. In addition, these entries include a wealth of practical tips — from shopping, restaurants and accommodation to important local addresses. Background information does not come up short either. You will find interesting information about the people and their culture as well as the regional geography, history and current political and economic situation.

As a particular service to our readers, *Practical Travel* includes prices in hard currencies so that they might gain a more accurate impression of prices even in countries with high rates of inflation. Most prices quoted in this book have been converted to US$ and £.

Accommodation

A current list of *hotels* including prices is published every six months by the Barbados Board of Tourism. Included in this are also apartments and cottages. The list is available free of charge by contacting the Barbados Board of Tourism *(→Tourist Information)* or the Barbados Hotel Association, P.O. Box 711C, Bridgetown, Barbados, Tel: 1-800-426-5041, Fax: (809) 429-2845.

Most hotels are in the middle and luxury classes and can be found clustered in and around the city. Especially the upper class hotels offer a number of recreational activities with a swimming pool setting the minimum standard.

Even during the summer, a hotel room cannot be had for under £17 ($35); during the winter, the prices are substantially higher.

In the centre of Bridgetown, there are a few *guest houses* charging less. These are, however, relatively simply furnished, appropriate for less demanding visitors. Addresses are available through the Tourism Board.

Youth Hostels: YMCA — Pinfold Street, Bridgetown, Tel: 426-3910; YWCA — Bradfield Country Road, St. Michael, Tel: 426-1240.

Dumfries, Henry's Lane, Lower Collymore Rock, St. Michael's, Tel: 426-1449.

Private Rooms: These are not plentiful and finding one can only be accomplished after arriving. One should check with the Board of Tourism *(→Tourist Information)*. The prices and standards of these rooms vary drastically.

Apartments: There are numerous apartment complexes along the southern and western coast of Barbados, equipped with self-catering kitchens. One should make sure that there is a refrigerator in the room and that the air-conditioning is not coin operated.

Prices during the summer range from £14 to £40 ($27 to $80) per night for a studio. The prices for apartments are also considerably higher during the winter.

The Barbados Board of Tourism also publishes a list of apartments with current prices.

Cottages: The accommodations within this category also include holiday apartments and houses, even though the Caribbean is not a classic destination for this type of lodging. The prices are somewhat higher than

the apartment complexes. Contacts and prices are listed in a brochure published by the Board of Tourism.
→*individual entries*

Airport

The Grantley Adams International Airport of Barbados is located in the district of Christ Church on the southern coast. It is around 18 kilometres (11¼ miles) from the capital city of Bridgetown (General Office Tel: 428-7101).

It was renovated in the 1970's and brought up to its present condition, an undertaking which cost millions. In addition to this, this airport is considered the most modern in the region and cannot only accommodate jumbo jets, but the Concorde as well.

As if painted by the artists hand: horses graze on a sandy pasture under the palm trees

Within the airport terminal is a branch office of the Tourist Board (Tel: 428-0937 and 428-5570); in addition, there are duty free shops, a restaurant, a currency exchange office and a police station which can take care of driving licence formalities *(→Travel Documents)*.

Grantley Adams International Airport is a four and a half hour flight from New York, five from Toronto, seven and a half from London and an eight and a half hour flight from Brussels and Frankfurt.

There is a taxi stand in front of the airport terminal with taxis available late into the night. The transfer by taxi to the most important towns and hotels along the southern and western coasts are subject to set fares — the taxis have no taxometer *(→Travel in Barbados)*. Taxis and buses at the airport are supervised by a special service. One merely states one's destination and is then given a slip of paper with the price on it. Then one proceeds to the waiting taxis.

For the trip to the western coast, one can count on paying £10 to £14 (US$ 20 to US$ 28); to the southern coast, £3 to £9 (US$ 6 to US$ 18). The airport tax (payable on departure) is 20 Barbados dollars at present. *→Travel in Barbados, Travelling to other Islands*

Andromeda Gardens *→Bathsheba*

Animal Flower Cave *↳North Point*

Animals and Wildlife

The natural fauna of the island includes only a limited number of animals. On Barbados, one will find rabbits living in the sugar cane fields, the rare Barbados apes imported long ago from Africa, and finally the mongooses which were imported years ago to keep the snake population in check, which had gone out of control. Within a short period of time, they had fulfilled their purpose and then some — the snake population was completely wiped out. As if that were not enough, the wild mongooses then began attacking domesticated chickens. Today, the mongooses are hunted.

The array of birds on Barbados is diverse, but not as colourful as one might expect: there are no wild parrots on Barbados.

The insects rarely reach plague proportions — they do exists but do not appear in swarms.

Domesticated animals include horses, donkeys, mules, cattle, pigs, goats, cats and dogs; in addition to this, poultry is also raised. Typical for the island are the black-bellied sheep, which are often mistaken for goats by tourists because of their short fur.

The fauna of the Caribbean Islands varies greatly from one island to the next. On the wooded islands (as for example Martinique) there are still some specimens of the poisonous snake species "fer de lance" — this is especially true for rain forest regions.

Archer's Bay

Archer's Bay, only a few miles southwest of →*North Point,* is considered one of the most picturesque and at the same time most untouched bays on the island. The sea churns amid the coastal cliffs; to the north is the adjacent Cluff's Bay. Archer's Bay can be reached from Bridgetown via Highway 1 to Speightstown and then continuing on Highway 1B until it ends. Then, following the rural road, keep right, heading north past Content. Around the police station in St. Lucy, turn left toward Grape Hall, Salmond which leads to Archer's Bay (St. Lucy district).

Ashford Bird Park

South of →*St. John's Church* is the privately operated Ashford Bird Park. Situated in the middle of a plantation, this is home to a wide variety of tropical birds in a beautiful setting.

The park is open during the entire year from 10 am to 5 pm; admission is presently Barbados $3.

In order to reach the Ashford Bird Park, one must take Highway 3 from Bridgetown to Market Hill, continuing on Highway 3B to Verdun / Small Hope, turning right onto the rural road. At the next crossing, turn right toward Ashford (St. John district).

Atlantis →*Maritime Attractions*

Barbados Wildlife Reserve

Directly near the →*Farley Hill National Park* (St. Peter district), Barbados operates a primate research centre where wild apes can be observed amid the lush vegetation of the Barbados Wildlife Reserve.

The Barbados Wildlife Reserve is open daily from 10 am to 5 pm, admission for adults is around £1.75 (US$ 3.35) and 85p (US$ 1.65) for children under twelve accompanied by at least one adult. (Tel: 422-8826). For directions from Bridgetown →*Farley Hill National Park*.

Bargaining

Bargaining is by no means the national pastime on Barbados. Here, it is not nearly as often the case that one can bargain with the prices as it is in other Caribbean countries. Bargaining is only appropriate at the fruit stands, with peddlers (for example on the beach) and in smaller shops with a more intimate atmosphere — and this, only with a pleasant smile, ample wit and charm; never stubborn or demanding.

The prices in the supermarkets and department stores are fixed — the same is of course true for restaurants.

Rum and the characteristic calypso rhythms: a colorful bar in Bridgetown — typically Caribbean

Bars

There are tiny bars very typical to the island along the streets especially in the population centres along the southern coast and in Bridgetown.
These are almost exclusively frequented by local residents, usually
housed in colourfully painted wooden huts and consisting only of a
makeshift bar with a few bar stools and a blaring radio. The bars open
at nightfall, which is always between 6 and 6:30 pm. They remain open
into the late night hours with calypso rhythms droning out onto the streets
and the guests sipping on rum punch — a favourite of the island
residents. This is the Caribbean atmosphere in its purest form without
any tourist influence.

In addition, there are bars belonging to the hotels which are not officially
only open to tourists, but tourists are in the majority due to the restric-
tive prices. For a cocktail, one must count on paying around £1.80

A street on the stormy eastern coast near Bathsbeba

(US$ 3.60); in more exclusive hotels, the prices are even higher. Some hotels offer happy hours from the afternoon until the early evening with drinks at half price.

Specialities in the hotel bars as well as the more traditional bars along the streets are various concoctions, usually based on rum — which is understandable since Barbados rum is famous worldwide.

The drinks cost only a few Barbados dollars in the street bars. These cost £2 to £7 (US$ 4 to US$ 14) in the hotels, but the hotel bars do offer a more elegant ambience.

In many of the bars along the streets, it is easy to start a conversation with the local residents; in others, the clientele prefer to be among themselves — tourists are considered an annoyance.

→*Cuisine*

Bathsheba

Bathsheba is a town known for its beautiful location slightly above the beaches along the eastern coast and because of its picturesque pastel coloured huts.

There is no tourist bustle in this fishing town, especially since the →*beaches* along the eastern coast are considered quite dangerous for swimming and due to the fact that the climate is more extreme. The town is exposed to the Atlantic side and is, therefore, subject to the strong trade winds.

Directly beyond the town is a series of rolling hills reaching elevations of up to 300 metres (980 feet) — in comparison, the highest mountain on the island is 340 metres (1,112 feet). The region surrounding Bathsheba is a popular getaway for the Barbadians, who own small cottages scattered around this region and spend their leisure time in this area. One reason for this is that it is cooler here than elsewhere on the island. Another is that overseas tourists come to this part of the island for a short excursion at most. A third reason is that the landscape is very beautiful.

Along the sandy beach are majestic rock monoliths, some of which are covered with moss.

Bathsheba / **Sights**

The town as a whole is definitely worth seeing with the hillsides in the background as well as the huts (mostly painted pink) and the monoliths. Counting among the attractions with local flair in Bathsheba is the tiny bar across from the large rock formation, slightly above the town along the coastal road. The complete selection of drinks of this bar is limited to the timeworn refrigerator filled with cola bottles. The real speciality are the tiny "baby bananas" — very aromatic and delicious; a delicacy costing only a few cents. The bar opens late in the afternoon and remains open as long as the proprietor sees fit.

Andromeda Gardens: In the beautiful terraced gardens, numerous exotic plants grow among the pools and cascades: for example, philodendrons, oleanders, sunflowers, bougainvillea, marsh-mallows, palm trees and ferns. Andromeda Gardens is located above the town of Bathsheba on Tent Bay (take the road to →*St. John's Church*). The gardens are open from 8 am until dusk; admission is between three and five Barbados dollars.

Bathsheba / **Practical Information**
Accommodation
Atlantis-Hotel, Tel: 433-9445.
Kingsley-Club, Tel: 433-9422.
Beaches and Swimming
Due to the strong currents off the coast in this area, it is not advisable to swim in the ocean here. Despite this, local residents do swim off the coast of Bathsheba, however, they are familiar with the local conditions (→*Beaches*).
Medical Care
Dr. P. Smith, Bathsheba, Tel: 433-9455.
Dr. Ian D. Smyth, Joe's River Plantation House, St. Joseph, Tel: 433-9499.
Restaurants
Bonito Bar & Diner, Bathsheba / St. Joseph, Tel: 433-9034.
Atlantis Hotel, Bathsheba / St. Joseph, Tel: 433-9445.
Transportation
Buses operate from Bridgetown to Bathsheba via Oistins; in addition there are the city-bypass buses from Bathsheba to Speightstown and connecting buses from there to Bridgetown.

Important Addresses
The police station in the St. Joseph District is in Castle Grant — located a couple of miles inland from Bethesda — and can be contacted by phoning the police central switchboard, Tel: 433-6600.

Beaches

A swim in the Caribbean — a dream even shared by land-lovers. A bounty of beautiful beaches with varying swimming conditions can be found all along the coastline of Barbados.

The western Caribbean coast of the island from Bridgetown all the way up to Archer's Bay offers magnificent, white and sheer endless beaches scattered with palm trees. The ocean floor has a gradual slope and also makes for excellent scuba diving.

The southern coastline from Bridgetown beyond Oistins is the ideal mix-

The beach near Oistins on the southern coast of the island — images of a tropical paradise

ture of the churning sea and beautiful beaches. As is the case in the northern extremes of the island, on the southern coast one will occasionally see where the Caribbean Sea meets up with the Atlantic Ocean, recognisable by the colours of the water. The green water of the Caribbean mingles with the blue tides of the Atlantic — an impressive contrast. Along the eastern coast — preferred by the local residents — the beaches are less suited to swimming: the Atlantic waves break on this coast and there is a dangerous undercurrent which is hard to recognise and difficult to judge. This undercurrent circulates the water under the surface in whirlpools. Tourists should forgo swimming on the eastern coast. On the other hand, this section of coastline is — like the others on the island — well suited for long walks.

Coastal cliffs almost continually from the area near the international airport near Paragon to Conset Point / St. John along the eastern coast

A rustic hut on a lonely trail — just one example of what Barbados has to offer when explored on foot

as well as from Gay's Cove to Cluff's Bay covering half of the coastline in the northernmost district of St. Lucy.

All of the beaches on the island are open to the public and free of charge. There are no beaches which belong exclusively to the hotels. Therefore, one will meet up with local residents everywhere, enjoying the beaches as much as the tourists. There are no lifeguards on the beaches of Barbados; therefore, if in unfamiliar waters, do not take any risks by swimming out too far. There are a number of peddlers on the beaches heavily frequented by tourists (→*Shopping, Bargaining*).

The beaches of Barbados are, as a general rule, very clean and it is expected that everyone does his or her part in maintaining this by not leaving behind any rubbish, beverage cans or the like. Beach chairs for rent are a rarity on Barbados. Equipment for aquatic sports is available to rent on various sections of the coast as well as on the beaches near the larger hotels or the beaches near more populated areas (→*Sports and Recreation*). On the sections of beach directly to the north and south of Bridgetown (Indian River / Brighton and Bay Estate) one will mainly see local residents. They usually prefer to be among themselves. Tourists should respect this and choose other beaches.

The beaches along the southern coast are relatively narrow and sometimes interrupted by cliffs, as is the case near Dover for instance. During the evening hours, various beaches are heavily populated by large, red crabs wielding their claws on their way inland — very interesting to observe.

The beaches along the western coast — also referred to as "the platinum coast" — are broader and more lively in regard to the entertainment offered. There are bars directly near the beach and it is more likely to find steel bands here than on the southern coast.

Remaining to be mentioned is Crane Bay with the Crane Beach Hotel and the Ginger Bay Hotel. This beach is one of the most beautiful on the entire island, despite the proximity of the coastal cliffs. The bay has snow-white sand, shimmering turquoise water, towering cliffs and swaying palm trees. It is accessible by way of a stairway from the Crane Beach Hotel built on the cliffs. In order to prevent the hotel from becoming a passageway for visitors to the beach, a fee of one to three Barbados dollars (depending on the season) is charged at the portal. If one decides to have a drink or a snack in the bar or the restaurant, then the fee for

access to the beach is included; one must merely present the bill stub.
Crane Bay is located in the St. Philip district near the town of Crane.
It is best reached via Highway 5 or 6 leading through the towns of Grove
and Sterling and up to Sandy Hill. From there, continue around one mile
using the secondary roads. Regardless of which beach, it is important
to spend only a limited amount of time exposed to the intense rays of
the sun at first and then increase exposure. The skin cannot withstand
more than ten minutes of unprotected exposure to the sun at first, considering that the rays are reflected by the water and the light coloured
sand. In addition, the stiff breeze makes it less noticeable if one already
has a sunburn.

Even if only strolling along the beach, one should wear a hat of some
kind (→*Clothing, Equipment, Medication*).

One should definitely choose a suntan lotion or oil with a high protection factor.

Finally, a piece of advice often given to guests by hotel porters and bar
keeper on setting out for the beach: "don't lie under the coconut trees"
— the coconuts could drop from a height of around 60 feet, which can
prove rather painful.

Beverages →*Cuisine*

Bicycle and Motorcycle Rental →*Car Rental*

Bridgetown

Barbados' capital city of Bridgetown on the southwestern coast is the
undisputed cultural, political and economical centre of the island. Almost
all shipping traffic to the island is handled in the harbour of Bridgetown.
The city has a population of over one hundred thousand and growing.
Bridgetown is most extensive along the southern coast: what were once
the towns of Hastings, Worthing and Maxwell are now part of the capitals
metropolitan area.

---

*The "Atlantis" submarine takes visitors on a sixty-minute trip into the
fascinating underwater world off the Barbadian coast* ▶

Bridgetown / **History**

One year after the first British settler landed in Jamestown (now Holetown) on the western coast, the Britons founded the city of Bridgetown in 1628 under the leadership of the Earl of Carlisle. It is said that they found a wooden bridge there, originating from the Indian population. According to legend, the Chamberlain Bridge spans the narrow Constitution River on the exact site where this bridge once stood.

The name Bridgetown is therefore not unfounded, but refers to the first construction found by the British settlers in the 17th century.

In competition with Holetown for the predominance on the island, Bridgetown won out, not lastly due to the more strategic location.

In 1961, five years before independence, Bridgetown was equipped with its deep-sea harbour at the southern entrance to town. This made it possible for Bridgetown to handle large freighters and also made it easier to handle the cruise ships. With the harbour, the leading role of Bridgetown as the capital city was also buttressed in the realm of international trade.

Bridgetown / **Sights**

"Atlantis": A ride in a submarine through the off-shore coral reef, departing from Bridgetown; for further information →*Maritime Attractions.*

Careenage: The Careenage is the municipal harbour of Bridgetown, located directly in the centre of the city and only a stone's throw from the parliamentary building (see Public Buildings below). To the north, the Careenage is bordered by the Chamberlain Bridge *(see below).* This harbour is especially worth seeing because of the jumble of boats which moor here and commute between the islands. Despite the peeling paint which leaves only traces of colour on the wooden planks, the Barbadian captains still set off to sea. The overall picture of the ships in the harbour against the backdrop of the modern shopping and bank buildings is definitely worth seeing. There are also two- and three-mast ships (like the Vanessa Ann) and catamarans which dock here — a station on their circuits between the Caribbean Islands. The boat to the Atlantis submarine departs from the northern banks of the Careenage (→*Maritime Attractions*).

At the entrance to the Careenage (across from Pelican Village) is the new fish market of Bridgetown. The largest fish market on the island, however, is found in →*Oistins*.

Chamberlain Bridge: This bridge spans the Constitution River at the mouth of the Careenage. The name Bridgetown refers to the Chamberlain Bridge's predecessor, a wooden bridge built by the Indians (→*Bridgetown/History*). The bridge is worth seeing, especially when considering the historical significance of this site.

The Fountain: With a rather uninspired name, this fountain beneath the palm trees on Trafalgar Square was built in 1865. Its shiny, smooth basin shimmers pink in the sunshine and is built from coral stone. The fountain was originally built as a monument to an engineering accomplishment — it commemorates the completion of the first water system in Bridgetown.

Garrison Savannah: The former parade and assembly square of the British colonial troops is now an important sports centre. Several times a year, horse races take place here and betting is permitted (→*Sports and Recreation*). In addition to these, the field in the middle of the Garrison Savannah is used by the local cricket teams for their matches. This complex is located at the southern entrance to Bridgetown, directly along Highway 7. At this location as well as at the northern side of Garrison Savannah are bus stops.

George Washington House: directly on Upper Bay Street is the two-storey George Washington House. Later to become president of the United States, George Washington lived here for several months with his brother Lawrence who was afflicted with leukemia.

Government House: In the eastern suburb of Belleville, a residential area for the affluent upper class, the Government Building is located on the corner of Belmont Road and Pine Road. This is the residence of the British governor general. He is the representative of the British Queen on the island of Barbados. This impressive building was constructed during the first century of British settlement of the island by a wealthy Quaker family before it became the permanent seat of the governor in 1702. It is not possible to see the interior.

Jolly Roger: An amusing cruise in a reproduction of a pirate ship departing from Bridgetown (→*Maritime Attractions*).

Museum: The island's National Museum is housed in what was formerly a military prison north of the Garrison Savanna. On display are relics from the islands history from the time of Indian dominance to the colonial period and up to the present. Exceptional pieces are the old maps and a copy of George Washington's writings about his visit to Barbados in 1751. In addition, the museum covers the island's flora and fauna, its industrial and cultural history. The museum's courtyard consists of a garden where one can take in the historical dance show "1627 and all that" twice weekly *(→Entertainment).*

The museum is open Monday to Saturday from 9 am to 6 pm (Tel: 427-0201 and 436-1956). Admission is 4 Barbados dollars; an alternative is a membership in the "Barbados Museum and Historical Society" for 400 Barbados dollars...

Nelson's Column: This monument, which shows the British Admiral Lord Nelson, is in the middle of the bustling Trafalgar Square *(see below).* In 1813, years before it's twin in London was erected, it was built by Richard Westmacott and installed on this square, which was formerly a park. Barbados is especially proud of the fact that this monument is a few years older than the world famous Nelson Monument in London.

Pelican Village: Pelican Village is the artisan village, built in the 1960's along the Princess Alice Highway in Bridgetown. The houses, which are both home, workshop and sales room to the artisans, can already be seen at quite a distance. They can be recognised by their deep brown colour and the pyramid shaped roofs.

For further information *→Shopping*

Public Buildings: The Public Buildings on Trafalgar Square house, in addition to the upper and lower houses of parliament *(→History, Politics),* a number of other municipal ministries and administration offices. These buildings can be seen from inside as long as one sticks to the office hours (usually from 9 am to noon). The tour through the parliamentary rooms in the east wing of the building is especially worth taking. These rooms have interesting stained glass windows depicting historical personalities of the British royal family, including Queen Victoria. Extensive renovations of the public buildings were recently completed.

This building — quite monumental for Caribbean standards — was built during the 1860's on the site of the old parliamentary building which was destroyed by a fire.

The entire architecture of this building is British in character (the tower is only one example), a building that could quite plausibly be found in England — albeit without the bright green shutters and the blossoming vegetation surrounding the building.

Visitor hours vary. It is best to ask at the Tourist Board *(→Tourist Information)* in Bridgetown for the exact time of tours through the building. These tours are subject to a nominal fee.

Queen's Park: Queen's Park is an extensive landscape of green with the Queen's Residence at its centre. This was the residence of the highest military officers of the British-West Indies troops up until shortly after the turn of the century. Today, it houses an occasional art exhibition or is used as a cultural centre (for theatre performances etc.). One curiosity in this extensive park is a massive baobab tree, which is over 1,000 years old according to recent research and also presents the Barbadian botanists with a puzzle: according to present knowledge, this species of tree did not grow in the Caribbean region at that time nor can prehistoric contact with Africa be proven.

Queen's Park is located at the northeastern entrance to Bridgetown and can best be reached from the central Trafalgar Square, walking past the Public Buildings and St. Michael's Cathedral *(see below)* and following St. Michael's Row and Constitution Road for about 600 yards.

St. Ann's Fort: Originally built in 1702 and continually modified in the following decades, St. Ann's Fort is situated across from the Garrison Savannah toward the sea. The most marked elements of this building are the signal tower and the guardhouse, on which the traces of a hurricane can still be seen. The fort is not open to the public, but Highway 7 runs directly by it making it possible to see a large portion of the fort.

Observatory: The astronomical research centre on Barbados is the Henry Bayley Observatory on Clapham Street. This small complex opened its doors in 1963 and is supported today by funding from the Barbados Astronomical Society. The observatory is less interesting than is the opportunity to view the stars from this vantage point near the equator. The Observatory is open to the public each Friday from 8:30 pm, closing usually around 10 or 11 pm.

St. Michael's Cathedral: This Anglican church was built in 1789 on the foundation of an older church which was victim of a hurricane. The same fate threatened the newer church as well when another hurricane swept

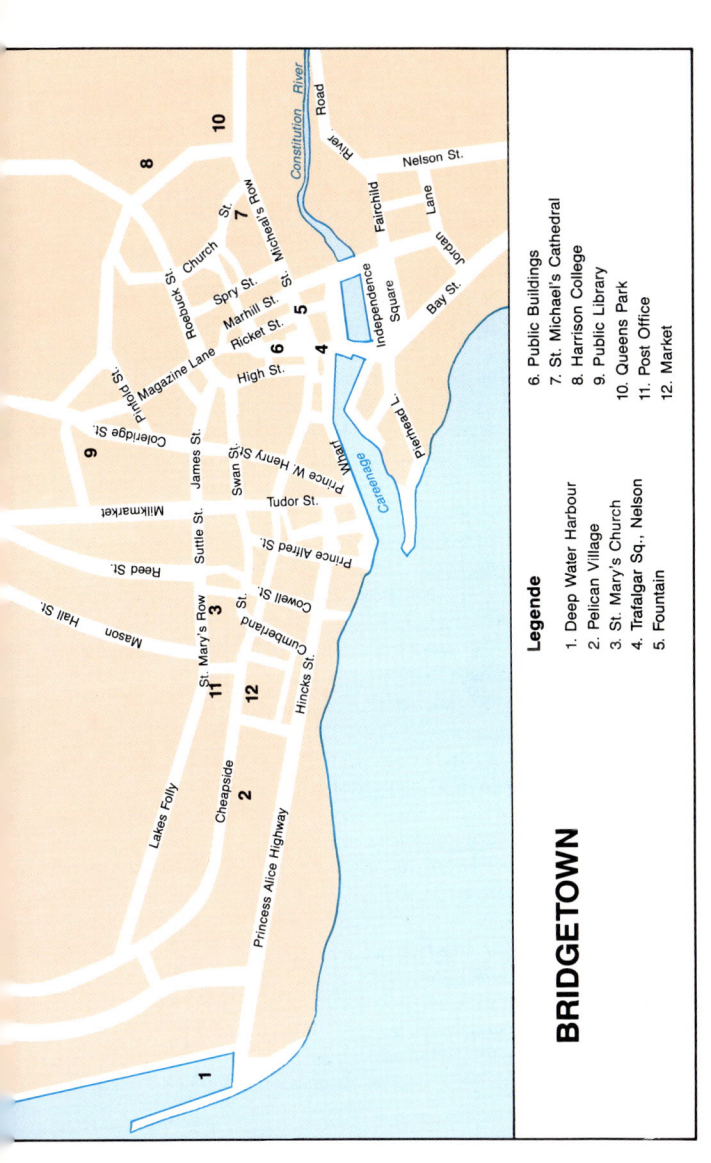

BRIDGETOWN

Legende

1. Deep Water Harbour
2. Pelican Village
3. St. Mary's Church
4. Trafalgar Sq., Nelson
5. Fountain
6. Public Buildings
7. St. Michael's Cathedral
8. Harrison College
9. Public Library
10. Queens Park
11. Post Office
12. Market

over the island: in 1831, the church was restored and brought to its present-day condition. The church is especially worth seeing for its typically Caribbean church architecture using coral rock as one of the main construction materials.

The baptismal font in the church's interior dates back to the middle of the 17th century.

The church can be visited during the day. When religious services are held, one should refrain from viewing the church.

Swan Street: The narrower Swan Street runs parallel to Victoria and Broad Streets; it is considered an exclusive shopping street by the local residents *(→Shopping)* and offers a colourful and lively atmosphere, resulting from the numerous peddlers, fruit stands with pyramids of coconuts etc. Many of the multi-storeyed houses along this street have large balconies which protrude over the street. These are reminiscent of the paintings, drawings, sketches and photographs of the 18th and 19th century.

Trafalgar Square: This is the central square in Bridgetown and one of the most lively places in town. At its centre is Nelson's Column; to one end, The Fountain. On one side of Trafalgar Square are the Public Buildings; to the other, the Careenage and the beginning of Broad Street, the city's shopping street. Thus, Trafalgar Square can be considered the heart of Bridgetown. At times fruit sellers sit here half buried by the selection of fruit they offer; sometimes painters also can be found here. There are bus stops as well as taxi stands on Trafalgar Square.

Bridgetown / **Practical Information**
Accommodation
Barbados Hilton Hotel, Needham's Point, Tel: 426-0200.
Grand Bay Beach Resort, Aquatic Gap, Tel: 426-0890.
Island Inn Hotel, Aquatic Gap, Tel: 436-6393.
Nautilus Beach Apartments, Bay Street, Tel: 426-3541.
→Accommodation, Camping
Banks
Bank of Credit and Commerce International Ltd., Broad Street, Tel: 429-2224.
Bank of Nova Scotia, Broad Street, Tel: 431-3000.
Barbados National Bank, James Street, Tel: 427-5920.

Barclays Bank International, Broad Street, Tel: 429-5151.
Canadian Imperial Bank of Commerce, Broad Street, Tel: 426-0571.
Caribbean Commercial Bank, Broad Street, Tel: 431-2500.
Royal Bank of Canada, Broad Street, Tel: 426-5200.
→*Money*

Beaches and Swimming

On the western as well as the southeastern edges of town are broad
beaches which are separated from the coastal road only by a narrow
greenbelt. These beaches are used predominantly by local residents
during their free time. They usually prefer to be among themselves here
and it is therefore advisable to make use of the beaches farther from
town or near the hotels where the tourist concentration is relatively high
anyway.

Car Rental

The car rental agencies are mainly on the outskirts of Bridgetown but
still in St. Michael district or in the district of Christ Church.
Listed below are only a few selected addresses:
Jones Garage Ltd., Pinfold Street and Passage Road, Tel: 426-4586 and
426-5030.
Mohammed Car Rentals, No.1 — 5th Avenue, Belleville, Tel: 426-3073.
(Numerous other addresses are listed in the yellow pages under
"Automobile Renting & Leasing").
It is recommended that one ask at the hotel reception for a recommen-
dation concerning car rental agencies because there are often
newcomers and others change management regularly.

Entertainment and Night Life

Various shows are offered in Bridgetown. For further information and
addresses and telephone numbers →*Entertainment*.
Cinemas: Globe Cinema, Upper Roebuck Street, Tel: 426-4692.
Globe Cinema Adamas Castle / Christ Church (Drive-in), Tel: 437-0479.
Olympic Theatre, High Street, Tel: 426-2009.
The current schedule for performances, for example in community cen-
tres or touring performances by international stars can be found in the
visitors' magazines (→*Tourist Information*).

Medical Care

There are excellent medical standards and specialists in Queen Elizabeth
Hospital, Tel: 436-6450. In addition to this, there are also private medical

and dental practices listed in the yellow pages. In Belleville, there is a dental clinic (Pine Road, Tel: 429-2617). It is also a good idea to ask for a recommendation from the hotel reception.

Restaurants

Listed here is only a selection of restaurants in and near Bridgetown, whereby one should not that some of the other regions along the southern coast have a higher concentration of good restaurants than Bridgetown.

"Brown Sugar" (Creole cuisine), Aquatic Gap, Highway 7, Tel: 426-7684.

"Barbados Hilton Hotel Restaurant," Needham's Point, Tel: 426-0200.

"The Pelican," Princess Alice Highway, Tel: 426-1966.

"Waterfront Café," Cavans Lane, Tel: 427-0093.

Shopping

The premiere shopping street in Bridgetown is the centrally located Broad Street. Here, one will find most of the department stores and the larger shops. Handicrafts are best purchased in Pelican Village *(→Shopping)*.

Sports and Recreation

The coastal hotels on the outskirts of Bridgetown offer a diverse programme of sports and recreation. In addition are also small, private entrepreneurs, who have established themselves in this market sector. For further information and addresses *→Sports and Recreation*. There are horse races and cricket matches at the Garrison Savannah *(→Sports and Recreation)*.

Transportation

There are taxi stands everywhere in Bridgetown. Almost all of the bus lines converge in Bridgetown as well. One must, however, pay attention to the fact that there are three different bus terminals in this city, each of which serves mainly the bus routes in a certain direction. For further information *→Travel in Barbados*.

Important Addresses

Police: Coleridge Street, Tel: 436-6600.

Tourist Information Office: Barbados Board of Tourism, Main Office, Harbour Road, Tel: 427-2623.

Buses →*Travel in Barbados*

Camping

Backpack tourists do not enjoy the best reputation in the Caribbean. They are not overly welcome on Barbados and must count on being scrutinised more closely than the other tourists upon arrival. Quite often, these type of tourists must offer proof that they can finance their stay on Barbados.

Camping area are virtually nonexistent on Barbados. Even camping on the beach is strictly prohibited, unlike most of the other islands of the Caribbean.

Car Rental

Prices on Barbados are quite high and the car rental agencies are no exception to this. Prices are usually given in US dollars. Most car rentals do not set their prices in this way because they want to avoid the problems of currency conversion — payment is really expected in US dollars. Those who would rather pay in Barbados $ will have to count on an unfavourable exchange rate.

One of the favourite rental car models among the tourists, and also one of the most widely available, is the "mini-moke" a hybrid of a jeep and the conventional compact car. Mini-mokes are usually roofless, but do sometimes include a removable roof which can be useful from July to November when short but heavy rain showers are quite common. There are no amenities like storage capacity or a locking glove box on these vehicles, making it wise to leave absolutely nothing in these cars while parked.

The rental price for this type of vehicle is around US$ 50 (£25) per day during the peak season (November to March). At other times, prices are slightly lower. The average daily price can be reduced by taking advantage of the special offers for rental periods lasting three, six or seven days.

During the peak season, it can happen that rental agencies might not even rent out a vehicle for only one day, if the demand is sufficiently high. At these times, the minimum rental period is three days. During the peak season, it is also well advised to book a rental car in conjunction with a hotel before arriving, especially when only planning a short stay on Barbados. Other than in these instances, Barbados does have a sufficient supply of rental cars as well as agencies, which are easy to find in the tourist centres clustered around the larger hotels. This is especially true for the southern coastal towns of Dover, St. Lawrence, Worthing, Hastings and Needham's Point where the Hilton Hotel is located. Avis has a branch office directly at the airport.

Those who opt for a standard car rather than a mini-moke, must calculate US$ 65 to US$ 85 (£33 to £43) per day and upwards into their travel budget. There are also discounts available for these vehicles — a weekly rental costs from US$ 200 (£100) to US$ 400 (£200). There are additional charges for insurance, and fuel also costs extra. Mileage is subject to varying calculations depending on the car rental agency, but as a general rule of thumb, one can count on a free mileage allowance of 300 miles per week. This is sufficient in most cases. Additional miles are charged at 20 to 30 cents (US) which should also be taken into consideration when planning more extensive trips on Barbados. One should definitely be sure to compare the prices and rental conditions of the various agencies on the island.

If in an accident where one is at fault, some car rental agencies require that the renter pay a portion of the damage. One should definitely ask about insurance conditions in advance.

As a general rule, drivers must be at least 21 years of age — some car rental agencies make exceptions to this rule seemingly arbitrarily, but don't count on this.

In addition to automobiles, it is also possible to rent a motorcycle by the week which costs from £54 to £84 ($107 to $167); sometimes this price also includes a helmet. In general, motorcycles and bicycles are becoming the trend — an increasing number of rental agencies include them in their selection, which also makes for lower prices. To find the best prices on the island, it is best to check with the hotel reception after arrival.

The daily rental fee for a bicycle averages around £4 to £5 ($8 to $10) and £20 to £25 ($40 to $50) per week.

Chalky Mount

Reaching an elevation of around 200 metres (655 feet), Chalky Mount is located in the southern regions of the island in the district of St. Andrew in the so-called →*Scotland District*. Chalky Mount is around 6 kilometres (4 miles) from →*Bathsheba*.

The Chalky Mount region is worth seeing for the tiny pottery village called "The Potteries" in which clay is formed by hand on the potter's wheel without the aid of any modern technology — techniques as they were practised hundreds of years ago.

The artisans usually do expect a tip from visitors who observe them at work. It is also possible to purchase the products. One does have the option to bargain with the prices within a certain range *(→Bargaining).* The Potteries are usually open from 9 am to 5 pm. Around noon, one will often find the potteries closed for lunch.

Chalky Mount itself is called the "sleeping Napoléon" due to its shape which, from a distance, is similar to a sleeping person with slightly curled-up legs. The Potteries and Chalky Mount are destinations offered by a number of tour organisers on the island.

Directions from Bridgetown: follow Highway 2 until shortly beyond Bruce Vale / St. Andrew (this is the junction of Highway 3A and Highway 2), directly thereafter near the small town of Haggatts, turn right onto the rural road and then left after a few hundred yards onto another rural road.

Cherry Tree Hill

Cherry Tree Hill, near the →*Nicholas Abbey* in the St. Andrew district, offers a beautiful view of the rolling hills of the →*Scotland District*. Cherry Tree Hill itself is around 250 metres (818 feet) high, an altitude only one hundred metres (330 feet) less than →*Mount Hillaby,* the highest elevation on the island.

Contrary to what one might expect from the name, there are no longer any cherry trees on Cherry Tree Hill. The street is lined with gnarled mahogany trees. One can occasionally spot a wild ape in this area as well.

Directions from Bridgetown: take Highway 1 via Holetown and Speightstown past the town of Mile and a Quarter; there, where the highway makes a sharp curve to the right, continue straight on the rural road passing Nicholas Abbey.

Cheques →*Money*

Children

Generally speaking, Barbados is well suited for a holiday with children. The hotels are equipped for the smaller guests; children's beds are available almost everywhere — these should, however, be booked in advance. The local residents are very open and friendly toward children. Along the western coastline, the beaches slope off gradually into the sea, making them safer for children. There are, however, no lifeguards patrolling the beaches *(→Beaches)*.

Climate

The climate on Barbados is constant during the entire year even though the months from June to November are considered the so-called "rainy season." However, this does not mean that rain pours from the sky for hours on end during the summer. Rain showers in the tropics are usually short and refreshing. Clouds quickly give way to the sun. Still, there are instances when it will rain an entire day — such days in one year can be counted on one hand, however. Longer rains are usually accompanied by "tropical waves" which can usually be seen during the months of August and September and can be the sign of a coming hurricane. Hurricanes form on the West African coast and move across the Atlantic to the Caribbean. Due to the geographical location of Barbados *(→Geography)* which is not aligned with the arch of the Antilles, Bar-

---

The sailing ship "Vanessa Ann" in the harbour of Bridgetown ▶

bados has remained untouched by hurricanes for a number of years. The early warning system is well developed, lowering the risks involved. If a hurricane approaches the coast, then airplanes and ships are warned by radio and diverted to other destinations. Most hurricanes dissolve over the sea, while during the winter months, hurricanes are more common.

The climate of Barbados is considered tropical in the classical sense — a lot of sun, short rain showers and high humidity.

This climate is considered optimal for those who suffer from rheumatism. The humidity is highest during the summer which is also true for the temperatures, reaching average highs from 28 to 30 °C (83 to 86 °F) which is around 2 to 3 degrees Celsius above the average highs during the winter months. Even during the nighttime, temperatures rarely drop below 20 °C (68 °F). Sunrise is between 5:30 to 6 am and sunset is between 6 and 6:30 pm.

The water temperature also remains constant from 22 to 25 °C (72 to 77 °F) during the entire year.

Climate Table

Month	1	2	3
January	77 (25)	75 (24)	14
February	79 (26)	77 (25)	10
March	81 (27)	77 (25)	10
April	84 (29)	79 (26)	8
May	86 (30)	79 (26)	9
June	86 (30)	79 (26)	16
July	86 (30)	81 (27)	18
August	86 (30)	79 (26)	17
September	84 (29)	79 (26)	16
October	82 (28)	79 (26)	15
November	82 (28)	77 (25)	16
December	79 (26)	77 (25)	15

1: Air temperature
2: Water temperature

3: Days with rain
Temperatures in °F (°C)

There are no regional fluctuations in regard to the climate on Barbados since the island is relatively flat. There are no mountain chains which affect the weather regionally. For this reason, if the weather is clear on the eastern coast then one can safely assume this will also be the case on the western coast.

Because of its flat landscape *(→Geography),* rain clouds — if there should happen to even be any — are swept over the island by the wind and then trapped by the volcanic mountains on neighbouring islands. With few exceptions, restaurants, hotel rooms and stores are air conditioned.

Clothing

Light cotton clothing is highly appropriate for Barbados since it is always pleasantly warm during the day — sometimes it is even too warm with a high level of humidity. Synthetic fabrics are less suited to this climate. Cotton polo shirts and t-shirts are ideal.

Since it is only slightly cooler during the evenings, warmer clothing is not necessary — at most, one might want to bring along a light cardigan sweater. A hat of some kind is a definite must for longer strolls. Women should remember that topless swimming and sunbathing is offensive to the local residents. Therefore, do not forget to pack a swimming suit.

In the leading hotels (for example "Sandy Lane" in St. James, Tel: 432-1311, one of the leading hotels of the world) evening attire is appropriate — a coat and tie for men and an elegant evening gown for women. This is also the case for the top restaurants. The hotel reception will be of help with information on the appropriate attire. One should definitely avoid wearing swimwear when in town. This is highly inappropriate for this island and the local residents react with embarrassment. Men should also wear a shirt. Shorts and shirts unbuttoned to the naval are highly inappropriate in restaurants.
→Equipment, Conduct

Codrington College

At the age of 34, Christopher Codrington founded this college in 1702 in the district of St. John near the boarder to the St. Philip district.

Originally, medicine and theology were taught here; today, the college
— built in the typically British architectural style and framed with palm
trees — is a seminary. An impressive road lined with palm trees up to
40 metres (130 feet) in height leads up to the main building. Behind the
building is a tropical garden which is very much worth seeing. Being
that the rooms are used for lectures, the interior of the building is not
open to the public; however, one is welcome to view the grounds.

At the time of its founding, this college was considered unique — individual Barbadian authors claim today that this is the "oldest institution for higher education" in the western world.

Christopher Codrington (1668-1710) was the governor of the Leeward
Islands, a plantation owner and quite liberal in overseeing his slaves.
Nearby Codrington College, somewhat inland, is the Codrington High
School, which is also built in the typically British architectural style.

*Lots of sun, short rain showers and high humidity — the tropical climate
of Barbados is stable during the entire year*

Directions from Bridgetown: take Highway 4 until it ends, then turn left onto a rural road. Turn right heading toward Sealy Hall at the next rural road and continue toward the sea to Codrington College. Another way is to take Highway 3 until it ends near →*St. John's Church.* Continue straight ahead on the rural road and further via Haynes Hill. Then from Cliff Cottage vial Coach Hill to Sealy Hall and from there, toward the sea to Codrington College.

Cole's Cave

The area surrounding this cave is characterised by tropical vegetation — quite unusual for Barbados. This makes even the trip itself to the cave a very pleasant experience. Cole's Cave itself is a cavern full of stalactites and stalagmites. These form individual rooms within the cave

The magnificent beach at Crane Bay in the southeastern portion of Barbados

with a ceiling height of up to five metres (16 feet). Streams flow through the caves as well and these are the habitat of cave crabs. The cave measures around 100 metres (110 yards) in length. The nearby cave network of Harrison's Cave is more developed in terms of tourism. The caves in the original coral layers of the island with their underground streams and rivers is physical evidence that there is ample freshwater circulation on the island, even though Barbados has next to no streams and rivers on its surface.

Directions from Bridgetown: take Highway 2 to Welchman Hall.

Conduct

The most important rule of conduct is to respect one's host and be aware of the cultural differences on Barbados. These differences include, in addition to other customs, a laid-back daily rhythm which one should not only accept but come to expect as well. One will have to wait, and demeaning comments will not help in this situation.

Finally, some points to note which are not acceptable:

— one should not take pictures of people without asking permission.

— one should be aware that beach and swimwear are for beaches and swimming pools — they are not acceptable for any other place.

Consulates →*Embassies*

Crane

The claim to fame of the tiny town of Crane on the eastern coast is its beautiful Crane Beach (→*Beaches*). The tourist infrastructure consists of two hotels.

From Bridgetown, Crane can be reached by taking Highway 5 or 6 via Grove and Sterling to Sandy Hill. From there, continue around one mile on the rural road (the way is marked).

Addresses: Crane Hotel Restaurant and Bar, Crane / St. Philip, Tel: 423-6220.

Ginger Bay Beach Club, Crane / St.Philip, Tel: 423-5810 (Ginger Bay is often closed during the summer months).

Credit Cards →*Money*

Crime

As is the case everywhere in the world, crime is also present on Barbados. However, the crime rate is one of the lowest in the entire Caribbean region.

Social tensions and the economic conditions can lead to increased incidence of crime, making it appropriate to be more cautious when touring certain areas of the cities.

One should be aware that all tourists — even students — are seen as being "wealthy" by the local residents. This is understandable when one considers that for local residents, financing a trans-Atlantic flight is simply out of the question. Also, many tourists spend more money in one day than a local resident earns in a week or even a month. This can of course provoke crime in the form of pickpockets.

The following are precautionary recommendations:

Never carry large sums of money. Use credit cards and traveller's cheques and deposit cash in the hotel safe.

One should not leave valuables lying around the hotel room and expensive jewellry should be left at home.

Never leave valuables in a rental car.

Never agree to transport parcels for strangers; one could unwittingly become involved in drug trafficking.

Never buy "underpriced" jewellry or other articles from street peddlers — these could be stolen goods.

If one is the victim of theft or any other crime, one should contact the police immediately. The official police report is essential for registering insurance claims.

When reading through these warnings and recommendations, the situation on Barbados might seem far more dramatic than it is. Keep in mind that these recommendations are generally applicable to everywhere in the world.

One final word of caution in regard to men on the beach asking if one is interested in cocaine or prostitutes. A clear "no" will conclude the dialogue. This is one unpleasant aspect of mass tourism. During the evenings, one should also avoid the area around the harbour and the red light district in Bridgetown.

→*Theft, Conduct, Police, Emergency*

Cruises →*Travelling to Barbados, Travelling to other Islands*

Cuisine

It is customary that a hotel will at least have a restaurant, whereby the smaller lodgings predominantly serve local cuisine. In the larger hotels, those which belong to international chains and the luxury hotels, there are usually a number of restaurants with international dishes among their repertoire. If a hotel does have a more than one restaurant, then one of these is usually buffet style with a broad range of tropical treats.

The outdoor restaurants are also very popular; these are usually directly outside a small bar. The only portion which does have a roof is the kitchen. These types of restaurants usually have a casual atmosphere and are often under the palm trees near the beach.

Even some of the aparthotels which include a kitchenette will often have very attractive restaurants.

In most of the restaurants, breakfast is only served to hotel guests. During all other meals, other visitors are welcome, whereby especially on the southern and western coast between Holetown and Speightstown, it is well-advised to make reservations.

There are a number of good as well as expensive restaurants especially on the southern coast between Dover and Needham's Point on Highway 7 and the roads branching off from it (Dover Road, St. Lawrence Coast Road etc.). These offer both Caribbean and international (American or European), Chinese and Italian cuisine (for example "Luigi's" on Dover Road).

The time breakfast is served in the hotels varies, but is usually from 7:30 to 10:30. If breakfast is not included in the package tour price, then one must count on paying from £3.50 to £5 ($7 to $10). Breakfast usually includes a number of fresh fruits from the region and wonderful juices — freshly pressed.

The times when the midday meal is served range from noon to 2 pm, as is customary in many other places. Many who enjoyed a large breakfast might not yet be hungry at this time and prefer the option of a siesta. This is at least the local custom, whereby at most a snack is eaten during midday and only rarely a hot meal. Still, more extensive lunches are served in some restaurants — these, usually in the larger hotels.

Around 4 pm — another relic of the British colonial times — teatime is announced. In addition to tea, fruit cocktails are also very popular as the first drink of the oncoming evening. Served with the drinks — whether hot or cold — is an array of fruits and biscuits.

With nightfall, between 6 and 6:30 pm, restaurants start serving dinner. It is usually served up until 10 o'clock.

Many hotels present "Caribbean Evenings" two or three evenings a week. This usually includes grilling outdoors, with specialities like flying fish and Creole pepperpot (see below). These are usually a self-service affair where everyone may enjoy as much as he or she wishes (usually around £7/$14, depending on the hotel).

Again, it is mostly the larger hotels which offer steel band music and folk dancers to round off these evenings.

One middle class hotel which is well known for its evening programmes is the "Southern Palms Beach Hotel" on St. Lawrence Coast Road. The absolute minimum for a meal, be it lunch or dinner, is £5 (US$ 10); there are also restaurants with prices well in excess of this.

For those on a tighter budget, or willing to forgo better cuisine, there are a number of fast food chains on the island.

It is also standard practice that a five percent governmental tax and ten percent service charge are added to the bill. This is, however, not the case if it is noted on the menu that the prices include these two surcharges.

Table manners are sooner European, where the knife and fork are held in the right and left hands respectively.

Foods

The ever-present evidence of the British culture on the island is not reflected in the foods. It is still possible to enjoy the variety of Caribbean cuisine on Barbados.

The foods of Barbados is characterised by a love of spices as well as for the unusual — demonstrating culinary creativity. Foods are usually heavily spiced — paprika, pepper and curry play a dominant role even today. There are also a number of speciality restaurants like Chinese, Vietnamese, Japanese, Indian, Mexican, Turkish, Greek, Yugoslavian and Italian. The Creole cuisine served on the island is also definitely recommended, offering a new type of dining experience. The names of these dishes will not say very much since they are relatively unknown in other parts of the world. The following in a brief overview of some of the most popular specialities, which can often be found on the menus:

Callalou: a soup made from leaves similar to spinach, a generous amount of garlic, onions, pepper, salt and coconut milk; sometimes with goat or crab meat; very spicy.

Christophene: a lightly sauteed squash.

Coo-coo: a corn meal casserole.

Dolphin: a tasty fish which has absolutely nothing to do with Flipper, and much smaller in comparison. There are a diversity of ways this fish is prepared.

Flying Fish: this is the speciality of all specialities served on Barbados. This fish has fins similar to wings and can "fly" by jumping out of the water and sailing for a number of yards. This fish is prepared in a number of ways; there are quite a few bones and this fish has a flavour similar to plaice. These fish can also be purchased in the duty-free area of the airport as a type of culinary souvenir (→*Shopping*).

Foo-Foo: a paste made from green cooking bananas and formed into dumplings; it is served warm and usually as a vegetable side dish. Tourists are usually puzzled by this food and it takes them a while to identify it.

Lambi: the meat from mussels, steamed and served cool.

Pastelles: corn and/or meat wrapped in banana leaves; served as an appetiser.

Pepperpot: a spicy stew of beef and chicken and a large proportion of vegetables. It is usually dark in colour and served in the traditional earthenware

Tan-Tan: Chicken liver marinated in brandy.

In addition to the above, there are a number of culinary variations on the banana. For example the bananas flambéed in rum and banana chips which are slices of green cooking bananas, deep fried and served as an appetiser or side dish.

Desserts

The desserts on Barbados are just as diverse as the main dishes; in contrast however, they are very sweet. Desserts usually make use of the fruits grown in the region with rum or fruit sherbet added to taste. However, the desserts focus on the coconut — whether the shell is used as the traditional dessert dish in which the fruits are served or in the form of coconut pudding or coconut ice cream (both of which are very sweet).

Beverages

The creativity of the Caribbean cuisine was already mentioned above — the diversity of the cocktails are no exception to this. Barbados is a virtual paradise for those who enjoy unusual and tasty cocktails with or without alcohol (but usually with).

Planter's Punch is a synonym for the Caribbean — a fruit cocktail with rum. Cocktails in hotels and restaurants cost from £1.75 to £7 (US$ 3 to US$ 14) *(→Bars),* whereby the non-alcoholic cocktails — sometimes fascinating fruit concoctions — are in the lower price range (up to £3.50/US$ 7).

Barbados also has its own brewery in St. Michael: Bank's Beer is served in most restaurants in addition to the expensive import beers. Bank's Beer is considered good by Caribbean standards and is very inexpensive. The international soft drinks like cola are also readily available, priced from £1 to £1.70 (US$ 2 to US$ 3.50) for a two or three litre bottle.

Mineral water is a rarity. This is due to the fact that the tap water on Barbados is of the highest quality. The islands is coral in origin, making the island itself a natural water filter. The result is that the tap water is even better than some bottled waters — refreshing and by all means a pleasure to drink.

Also worth mentioning is a drink typical to the island — the so-called "Mauby," an inexpensive extract from the bark and roots of various plants with spices (like cinnamon) added to it. Definitely an acquired taste.

With the exception of rum, liquor and wines are quite expensive on the island, which is understandable since the largest proportion of these are imported from abroad.

The national drink is of course Barbados rum, which is among the most widely known in the world along with the Jamaican. It is inexpensive everywhere — even in the restaurants — and also makes a nice souvenir. However, be aware of customs regulations before purchasing large amounts of rum. Local residents drink their rum with cola, with tap water or merely pure.

Caution is advised in regard to rum, other alcoholic beverages and even beer: one could have problems with the effects of alcohol in the tropical heat of Barbados. Thus, the same is true for alcohol as is for exposure to the sun. Be cautious at first. There have been tourists who first discovered their love of rum on the island and subsequently experienced little else that the island has to offer.

Culture

Cultural life on the island of Barbados has a number of interesting aspects. This is mainly due to the high standards of education on the island.

In the lobbies of the larger hotels (the Hilton for example) there are quite often art exhibitions. This is also true for the small galleries and handicrafts workshops in Pelican Village (→*Shopping*).

The Barbados Board of Tourism has a brochure with the addresses and telephone numbers of the larger galleries (→*Tourist Information*).

The schedule for cultural events like cinemas, theatre performances, international groups and bands etc. are listed in the visitor magazines published every 14 days (→*Tourist Information*).

Interesting auctions also take place occasionally, with antique furnishings from the colonial period (dates and times are listed in the daily newspapers (→*Newspapers and Magazines*).

One especially interesting cultural attraction on the island is the Barbados Museum, where a collection of various articles documenting the history of the island can be seen (→*Bridgetown*).

Unlike other places, cultural life is characterised by spontaneity which makes for a fresh and appealing approach to the arts.

Currency →*Money*

Customs and Traditions →*Holidays and Celebrations, Folklore, Cuisine, Culture, People*

Customs Regulations

All objects brought into the country are subject to duty. The exceptions to this are the following: articles for personal use including photographic and sports equipment; the duty free limits for alcohol and tobacco are one litre of liquor and 50 cigars or 200 cigarettes.

Upon departure, an airport tax is levied in the amount of 20 Barbados dollars — this is paid upon checking in and proof of payment must be shown to the customs officers at the passport control.

Diplomatic Representation →*Embassies*

Discounts

As a general rule, one can safely say that a holiday on Barbados is expensive — discounts are rare. In the low season from April to November, however, the hotel prices and airfares are substantially lower in comparison to the winter, with hotel prices reduced as much as 50%. Other ways to save money are included under the headings *Travelling to Barbados* and *Travelling to other Islands*.

Dover, Maxwell, St. Lawrence

The towns of Dover, Maxwell and St. Lawrence on the southern coast are similar to →*Hastings* and →*Worthing* in that they can be considered suburbs of →*Bridgetown*. These towns are all interconnected and the borders of each are hardly recognisable.

Concentrated in this area is the tourist region of the southern coast. With the exception of the water and the beaches, there are few sights worth mentioning. What is worth seeing are the colourful houses lining the streets leading inland.

Dover, Maxwell, St. Lawrence / **Practical Information**
Accommodation
Andrea on-the-sea Hotel, St. Lawrence, Tel: 428-6021.
Casuarina Beach Club, Dover, Tel: 428-3600.
Divi Southwinds Hotel & Beach Club, St. Lawrence, Tel: 428-7181.
Dover Beach Apartment Hotel, St. Lawrence, Tel: 428-8076.
Fairholm Hotel and Apartments, Maxwell, Tel: 428-9425.
Half Moon Beach Hotel, St. Lawrence Gap, Tel: 428-7131.
Rainbow Reef Hotel, Dover, Tel: 428-5110.
Sand Acres Beach Club, Maxwell Coast, Tel: 428-7234.
Sea Breeze Aparthotel, Maxwell Coast Road, Tel: 428-2825.
Shangri-La Apartment Hotel, Maxwell Coast, Tel: 428-9112.
Southern Palms Beach Club, St. Lawrence Gap, Tel: 428-7171.

Spinnakers Hotel, Bar & Restaurant, St. Lawrence Gap, Tel: 428-7308.
Banks
Barclays Bank, St. Lawrence, Tel: 428-7452.
Beaches
Swimming conditions along the southern coast are quite good, but the beaches are substantially narrower than along the western coast and they are occasionally interrupted by coastal cliffs (→*Beaches)*.
Car Rental
M. Jay's Rentals Ltd., St. Lawrence Gap, Tel: 428-7319.
Entertainment and Night Life →*Entertainment*
Restaurants
The following is a selection from the large selection of various kinds of restaurants within the southern coastal region of Dover, Maxwell and St. Lawrence:

Boomer's Guest House & Restaurant, St. Lawrence, Tel: 428-8439.

Captain's Carvery, The Ship Inn, St. Lawrence Gap, Tel: 435-6961.

Luigi's Restaurant, Dover, Tel: 428-9218.

Melting Pot Restaurant, St. Lawrence Main Road, Tel: 428-3555.

Pisces Restaurant, St. Lawrence Gap, Tel: 435-6564.

Plantation Restaurant, St. Lawrence Road, Tel: 428-5048.

Southern Palms Beach Club, Khus Khus Bar & Restaurant, St. Lawrence, Tel: 428-7171.

Steak House, St. Lawrence Gap, Tel: 428-7152.

Witch Doctor, St. Lawrence, Tel: 435-6581.
Shopping
There are a number of smaller supermarkets and shops; often, one can also find peddlers selling fruits and vegetables. The nearest large department stores can be found in Hastings or in Oistins in the opposite direction.
Sports and Recreation
There are numerous opportunities and facilities for sports and recreation in this area. This is especially true for aquatic sports. For further information →*Sports and Recreation.*
Transportation
There are bus stops for buses headed toward both Bridgetown and Oistins lined along Highway 7. The streets along the coast are in very

good repair. Those driving themselves should be careful when parking near the hotel: in these areas there are often speed bumps which can be easily overlooked.

Important Addresses

The police station for the southern coastal district is located between Worthing and St. Lawrence. As is the case with all police stations on the island, the police can be contacted by dialling the number 436-6600.

Drax Hall

Drax Hall in the St. George district is one of the oldest preserved plantation manor houses from the early period of the British settlement. Today, it is privately owned. It was built around 1650 by the farmer James Drax.

The estate can be toured for a small fee, and this at varying times during the winter months. It houses interesting colonial furnishings as well as an impressive staircase. During the summer, one only rarely has the opportunity to visit Drax Hall. The exact times for visiting Drax Hall are available from the Tourist Board (→ *Tourist Information*) or directly at Drax Hall Plantation; St. George, Tel: 433-1240.

Directions from Bridgetown: take Highway 4 via Constant and Mount to Drax Hall.

Driving Licence → *Travel Documents*

Duty-Free Shopping → *Shopping*

Economy

The main economic factor of Barbados is without question agriculture. The most important crop is sugar cane — the most important component of Barbados' export goods, the Barbados Rum.

Other important agricultural products are coconuts and breadfruit.

The most important source of hard currencies is the tourist industry. The number of people employed either directly or indirectly in this industrial sector is over 30,000.

There is active trade between the Caribbean members of the CARICOM organisation. What one island cannot produce is provided by the other.

Electricity

The electrical voltage on the island is 110 volt (50 Hz) alternating current. The island has both the British tripolar sockets and the American standard sockets. Adaptors might be necessary. Many hotels will have the appropriate adaptors available for their guests upon request, but one cannot count on this.

The electrical supply itself is dependable.

Embassies and Diplomatic Representation

British High Commission
Lower Collymore Rock
St Michael, Barbados
Tel: (809) 436-6694

Canadian High Commission
Bishop Court Hill
St. Michael, Barbados
Tel: (809) 429-3550

United States Embassy
Consular Section, 1st Floor
Trident House
Bridgetown, Barbados
Tel: (809) 436-4950

Emergency

If involved in an automobile accident, one should report this to the police even if there are no injuries for insurance purposes.

In any emergency in the hotel, contact the reception, which can organise everything quickly. They can arrange for a nearby doctor to come immediately since it takes a while for an ambulance to arrive since ambulances must navigate the heavy traffic on the island and they are also relatively few in number.

The following telephone numbers will be of help in an emergency situation:

Police (emergency number): 112
Fire Department: 113
Ambulance: 426-1113
Queen Elizabeth Hospital in Bridgetown: 436-6450
Coast Guard (emergency number): 427-8819.

When calling from a hotel room, please note that one must often first dial a zero for an outside line.
→*Police, Medical Care*

Entering Barbados →*Travel Documents, Customs Regulations*

The sweet life: an elegant villa snuggled in the lush vegetation and directly on the beach

Entertainment

Night life on Barbados is diverse: night clubs, discotheques, →*bars* and pubs. Moonlight is the backdrop for evening picnics on the beach and parties on the cruise ships. Hotels and night clubs offer a special attraction with calypso, limbo and fire dancers as well as folk music and the rhythms of the steel band.

Barbados quiets down in the early evening — the chance for a short rest before diving into the night life.

Night clubs are concentrated along the southern coast and in the capital city of Bridgetown. The programme consists mainly of dance spectacles and variety performers. One of the most widely known club is "The Plantation Restaurant & Garden Theatre" in the southern district of Christ Church (St. Lawrence, Tel: 428-5048 or 428-2986). On Monday, Wednesday, Friday and Saturday, two different shows are presented consisting of limbo, reggae, samba, and a number of fast-paced surprises. The price for the show including dinner, drinks and hotel transfer is £20 (US$ 40).

Other dinner shows are:

"1627 And All That": a tour through the Barbados Museum north of the Garrison Savannah, two historical Afro-Caribbean dance performances, appetiser, a traditional Caribbean buffet, drinks and hotel transfer. The price is also £20 (US$ 40). Reservations can be made by contacting Tel: 435-6900. This takes place on Thursdays and Sundays from 6:30 to 11 pm.

"Barbados Barbados": Boiling House Balls Estate, Christ Church, reservations can also be made by contacting Tel: 435-6900. This is the performance of a historical comedy in two acts. The price of £20 (US$ 40) includes appetisers, a typically Caribbean buffet, drinks and hotel transfer. Performances Tuesday from 6:30 to 11 pm.

Night Club Xanadu in the Ocean View Hotel, Hastings / Christ Church, Tel: 427-7821. Cabaret and variety performances, seafood buffet. Performances on Thursdays; price: £20 (US$ 40).

Reservations are recommended for all of the above performances, especially considering that the prices include hotel transfer.

In addition to the dinner performances, entertainment is also offered in many of the larger hotels (→*Cuisine*).

British style night clubs, discotheques and pubs are:

The Flambeau / Barbados Hilton Hotel, Needham's Point, Tel: 426-0200.

Bel Air Jazz Club, Bay Street, Tel: 436-1664.

The Coach House, Paynes Bay / St. James, Tel: 432-1163.

Heywood's, St. Peter, Tel: 422-4900.

Ship Inn, St. Lawrence Gap / Christ Church, Tel: 435-6961.

→*Bars*

Equipment

Barbados is not an island which requires any special type of equipment. Those who plan on taking part in any recreational activities like scuba diving are best advised to bring along their equipment or at least part of it. It is rather expensive to rent this type of gear on Barbados.

As an orientation, the following are a few examples of prices:

A surfboard will cost from £5 to £7 ($10 to $15) per hour and £14 to £17 ($27 to $35) per day. For a scuba diving excursion, on must count on paying around £20 to £27 ($40 to $54) including equipment — even the use of the decompression chamber.

One thing that should not be missing in anyone's luggage is a hat or scarf to protect against the intense sunshine. Also suntan lotion with a high protection factor is imperative. Medications taken on a regular basis should be brought along in sufficient quantities, especially those which require a prescription.

Excursions

As is the case with any tourist destination, organised excursions are offered to every point of interest on Barbados, to other islands and even to the South American mainland (especially to Caracas). Prices for these are usually in US dollars and not in Barbados dollars. One should definitely be aware of this fact when comparing prices. Some tour organisers offer half-day excursions accompanied by a tour guide covering the entire island. These tours are, however, not always recommendable because they only take visitors to the most widely known attractions and offer little insight into the islands "secrets." These are good in giving an orientation of the island or as a short diversion for those who plan on spending most of their time at the beach.

On occasion, there are also more extensive full-day tours arranged by local tour agencies. It can be worthwhile to check with the tourist information office *(→Tourist Information)*. The chances of finding such a tour are better in the winter than during the summer. One should be wary of tour organisations which advertise half-price offers for popular tours with the "Atlantis" submarine or the "Jolly Roger" pirate ship *(→Maritime Attractions)*. These are usually tours for marketing condominiums or time-sharing on the island.

→Travel in Barbados, Traveling to other Islands, Maritime Attractions, Tourist Information

Exit Ticket *→Travel Documents*

Farley Hill National Park

There is an especially impressive view of the rugged *→Scotland District* plateau from Farley Hill National Park. This national park was formerly the gardens of a plantation.

Among the vegetation represented here today include, in addition to palm trees and tropical fruit trees, a number of woods like mahogany.

The national park is a recreational area and not — as might be assumed from the name — a nature reserve. Facilities like picnic areas have been added to various areas of the park.

Towering high above the community of St. Peter are the ruins of the Farley Hill manor house. It was here that the owner Sir Graham Briggs received the later King George V and also the setting for the successful film "Island in the Sun." In 1965, the manor house fell victim to a fire — one year later, Queen Elizabeth unveiled a commemorative plaque on this site.

Directions from Bridgetown: take Highway 1 along the western Caribbean coast via Holetown and Speightstown to Welchtown / Farley Hill Park. One must pay special attention in Speightstown, because the Highway branches off here to Highway 1B. Do not be confused by the fact that Highway 1 suddenly becomes Highway 2 shortly beyond Farley Hill. These two Highways meet at this point. The western side of the loop is Highway 1 and the eastern is Highway 2 leading back to Bridgetown.

→Barbados Wildlife Reserve

Folklore

The are no traditional costumes especially typical of Barbados. What is worn is anything that is light and airy — anything practical for the tropical climate.

"Caribbean Folk Music" began its conquest of the world years ago. People on all five continents dance to the rhythms of limbo, reggae and calypso music, and this especially where this music originated: in the Caribbean and therefore also on Barbados. The origin of this music lies with the tens of thousands of black Africans who were brought to the new world from West Africa for the slave trade. Many of the rhythms and the ecstatic dances had religious significance. The arrival in the Caribbean brought the acquaintance of new musical instruments and with intonated chorales, particularly the result of contact with Catholic missionaries.

The sounds of the Caribbean: a steel band musician in action

The Caribbean music is a mixture of these influences. This music often served as the only means for the slaves to maintain a connection with their homeland. The rhythms brought a feeling of belonging, bonded the black population together and became an expression of protest. Calypso always had flippant and amusing texts, structured like a ballad. Limbo, in contrast, was originally rooted in a specific cult.

The talent for improvisation is also apparent in the choice of musical instruments, even though the famous steel bands first came into being after the Second World War. The number of musicians in the band can vary from six to several hundred at especially large celebrations. The origin of the instrument can best be described by the old adage "necessity it the mother of invention." Oil barrels were transformed into musical instruments. Even today, a car top will suffice as an instrument for a rhythm that just needs to get out. Music of the Caribbean is by no means uniform. While Barbados is characterised by the standard forms of calypso, limbo and reggae, other islands have developed other forms: benguine on Martinique and (less often) Guadeloupe, tambu on Curaçao, goombay on the Bahamas and so on.

Dances are quick-paced with the emphasis here on improvisation as well and not on structured dance steps. Limbo — at least among the local experts — is danced under a burning rod only several inches above the ground. One can experience this either by coincidence on the beach or in many places, during the regional festivals. If one does not have as much luck, then the night clubs are a viable alternative, where the limbo is danced during the entire year.

Fuel

Fuel on the island of Barbados is of good quality and will prove to be no problem for any of the rental cars. Fuel is supplied to Barbados mainly from the oil exporting countries of South and Central America (Venezuela, Mexico etc.). Per litre, one can count on paying around 40p (80 US cents).
→Car Rental

Geography

Barbados is the easternmost islands offset from the Antilles, which stretch in an arch from Cuba to Aruba. The eastern coast of the island is predominantly rocky and is visible evidence of the power of the Atlantic waves. In contrast, the western coast slopes gradually into the Caribbean Sea with magnificent sandy beaches.

The highest elevation on this pear-shaped island is only 340 metres (1,112 feet) in altitude. The island itself has an area of 431 square kilometres (168 square miles). There are no mountain chains on this flat island nor are there any rivers on the surface of the island, with the exception of a few small streams. However, below the surface of the island, the water circulates in large rivers in the underground network of caves. This is an explanation for names like River Road, Indian River and River Bay. In contrast to the mountainous neighbouring islands of volcanic origin, Barbados was formed by coral deposits. The sand on the beaches also originates from eroded coral.

This subterranean coral base of the island is up to 100 metres (327 feet) thick in some places and makes the island itself a type of natural water filter. The water is very pure on Barbados.

The island with its capital city of Bridgetown on the southwestern coast is divided into eleven districts: St. Michael, Christ Church, St. Philip, St. John, St. George, St. Joseph, St. Andrew, St. Peter, St. Lucy, St. James and St. Thomas. The districts of St. Thomas and St. George are the only two districts which do not include coastline. With the exception of the four large cities of Bridgetown (with a population of 100,000, this is home to over a third of the total population of Barbados), Holetown, Speightstown and Oistins, the towns on Barbados are very small and often consist of only a few houses. For this reason, this travel guide concentrates on the four large cities and other points of interest.

The southern coast especially has developed into one heavily populated metropolitan area including the towns of Hastings, Worthing and Dover. The nearest island is St. Lucia, which is around 160 kilometres (100 miles) from Barbados.

Greetings

The Barbadians are very open and friendly: they will smile and greet visitors with a friendly hello or hi even if they are complete strangers. Visitors will find this adds a very pleasant touch to the holiday atmosphere of the island.

Gun Hill

Earlier, Gun Hill in the district of St. George played an important role in the defence of the island. From this summit, messages were sent via a signal station to St. Ann's Fort *(→Bridgetown)*. In the middle of the past century, British soldiers carved a figure of a lion from the rocks. Directions from Bridgetown: take Highway 4 past Newmarket and turn left shortly beyond the town onto the rural road. Continue past Constant, Rectory and Walkers to Gun Hill in the middle of the triangle formed by Francia, Salisbury and Hilbury.

Harrison's Cave

Harrison's Cave is the most developed cave in terms of tourism. It is located at the approximate geographic centre of Barbados in the St. Thomas district. A small train takes visitors along the underground rivers through the extensive network of caverns with interesting lighting effects. The tour programme is conceived so that one first visits the small exhibition on the surface with a display of Arawak Indian tools *(→History)*. It is assumed that some of these native inhabitants of the island lived in Harrison's Cave. After a brief introductory slide show, the trip with the electric train begins. At the deepest point of the cave, one can get out of the train and walk to a waterfall which plunges from a height of around 14 metres (46 feet). The tour of the cave is around one mile in length.

Group tours are offered only with advance notice (Tel: 438-6640, 41, 43, 44 and 45). The first tour begins daily at 9 am; the last, at 4 pm. There is a small fee for admission. Tour organisers like Caribbean Safari Tours (Tel: 427-5100) offer organised tours to Harrison's Cave and "Flower Forest" including hotel transfer, priced at around £13 (US$ 25). The trip is much less expensive when travelling on one's own.

Directions from Bridgetown: take Highway 2 past the town of Ayshford toward Welchman Hall. Shortly before reaching Welchman Hall, turn right. The way is marked.

→Cole's Cave

Hastings

Hastings is a beach resort with a good tourist infrastructure much like the towns of Rockley, →*Worthing,* St. Lawrence and Maxwell. However, as is the case with almost every other tourist centre on the island, no high rise hotels also have been added to the landscape. Geographically speaking, this small town in the southern district of Christ Church is virtually a suburb of Bridgetown. There is no marked distinction between Bridgetown and Hastings.

Hastings / **Practical Information**
Accommodation
Hotels and apartment houses in Hastings and Rockley (inclusion in this list does not constitute a recommendation):

The coral base of Barbados makes for an ideal natural filter for the drinking water

Abbeville Hotel & Bert's Bar, Rockley, Tel: 435-7974.

Accra Beach Hotel, Rockley, Tel: 435-8920.

Asta Apartment Hotel, Palm Beach, Hastings, Tel: 427-2541.

Caribbee Beach Hotel, Hastings, Tel: 436-6232.

Coconut Court Beach Apartments, Hastings, Tel: 427-1655.

Flamboyant Hotel, Hastings, Tel: 427-5588.

Pirate's Inn Hotel, Hastings, Tel: 426-6273.

Regency Cove Hotel, Hastings, Tel: 435-8924.

Riviera Apartment Hotel, Rockley Beach, Tel: 435-8970.

Rockley Resort & Beach Club, Rockley, Tel: 435-7880.

Sea View Hotel, Hastings, Tel: 426-1450.

Sunshine Beach Apartments, Hastings, Tel: 427-1234.

Woodville Beach Apartments, Hastings, Tel: 435-6694.

Banks

Royal Bank of Canada, Hastings Branch, Tel: 427-7740.

It is only a short walk to the main bank offices in Bridgetown.

Beaches

The beach along the southern coast offers excellent swimming directly below the hotels or below Highway 7. These sections of beaches are also relatively heavily frequented by the local residents.

Car Rental →*Bridgetown*

Medical Care

There are several medical practices in Hastings and good public transportation to Bridgetown where one has access to numerous medical facilities. In the case that medical attention should be necessary, it is best to first contact the hotel reception or the Queen Elizabeth Hospital in Bridgetown (Tel: 436-6450).

Restaurants

Restaurants in Hastings and along the adjacent Rockley Beach:

Caribbee Beach Hotel Restaurant, Hastings, Tel: 436-6232.

Da Luciano, Hastings, Tel: 427-5518.

Flamboyant, Hastings, Tel: 427-5588.

Golden Beach Apartel Restaurant, Hastings, Tel: 426-6784.

Ocean View Hotel Restaurant, Hastings, Tel: 427-7821.

Rockley Resort & Beach Club Restaurant, Tel: 435-7880.

Virginian Restaurant, Hastings (Hotel Seaview), Tel: 427-7963.

Shopping

There are a number of supermarkets in Hastings, which are especially of interest for those who choose to cook their own meals in the apartment complexes. The department store chain Cave Shepherd has a store directly on Highway 7.

Sports and Recreation

There are a number of sports and recreational activities offered by the hotels. The addresses of sports equipment rentals are listed under the heading →*Sports and Recreation.*

Transportation

There are good and convenient bus connections from Hastings via Bridgetown or Oistins to every larger town on the island. Buses depart from the bus stops along Highway 7.

Health Insurance

It is recommended to take out a supplemental health insurance policy for the duration of one's trip to Barbados. The way this functions on Barbados is that one pays directly for treatment and medication and this is then reimbursed by one's health insurance company upon returning home. Therefore, always request a detailed invoice for any treatment or medication, including the diagnosis type of treatment.

Those with comprehensive health insurance coverage should check with their health insurance company to find out if existing coverage applies to foreign travel.

History

Originally, Barbados was inhabited by Carib Indians, after which the archipelago was named. They were said to have reached the island in the 14th century from South America and enslaved the Arawak Indians who lived on Barbados up until that time.

When the Portuguese discovered the island in 1536, only a few of the Carib Indians and none of the Arawak Indians remained. It is speculated that it was much easier to reach the other islands of the region because of the constant northeasterly trade winds than to sail 100 miles from St. Vincent to Barbados against the wind. Owing to this, Barbados might have been forgotten, while the remaining population decided to leave the islands successively.

The Portuguese seafarers did not claim the island for themselves — they had their sights set on Brazil. However, they did name the island: Isla de los Barbados — the bearded island, after the bearded fig trees growing near the coast. It was first in 1625 that the English merchant John Powell took possession of the island for the English crown — an island which was completely uninhabited by this time.

Two years later, eighty settlers landed on the western coast, having been motivated to this journey by John Powell's employer, the merchant Sir William Courteen. Today, a commemorative plaque marks the site of this landing in Holetown, originally founded by the settlers as Jamestown. English law and political institutions were quickly established on Barbados, making it known as "little England" after only a short time. The first parliament (→Politics) convened in 1639, only twelve years after the first settlers landed. The 350th anniversary of the parliament was celebrated extravagantly in 1989. During the rule of Oliver Cromwell, the Barbadians questioned strict loyalty to the English monarchy. In 1651, Cromwell sent armed forces and the islander's surrendered in 1652 near Mermaid Tavern (Oistins in Christ Church today). It was this contract of surrendered which was the forerunner of the constitution. It was the contract of surrender which guaranteed the right to extensive autonomy and an elected lower house. Thus, what was actually a defeat was still a victory.

In 1831, free blacks were given the right to vote and in 1834, slavery was abolished. In 1840, the former slaves were given full rights as citizens. In 1924, the first black political organisation was founded, the "Democratic League." In 1951, the first representative government took office. This was the first government to be elected after the general right to vote for all adults was enacted.

On November 30, 1966, Barbados was awarded its independence from the British colonial government (→Holidays and Celebrations). Today, the Barbados is considered the most politically stable state in the region, there is a relatively high standard of living, the island is economically successful and the level of education is high.

Barbados is the only island in the archipelago which was British during its entire colonial period. On other islands there were often battles between the European imperial powers to which the civil population often fell victim. Such problems hindered the development of infrastructures on many of the islands as a basis for a higher standard of living — problems Barbados did not have.

Barbados is still proud of its most prominent visitor George Washington, who came to the island in 1751 with his brother Lawrence who suffered from leukemia. Historians who have studied the history of Barbados consider it possible that George Washington studied the Barbadian constitution at this time. It is said that there are certain parallells to the preamble of the US Constitution, written later.

Holetown

Thanks to its magnificent beaches bordering on the turquoise waters of the Caribbean Sea, Holetown has developed into a preferred holiday beach resort. Hotels and apartment complexes line the coast far beyond the city limits to the north and south.

The town itself is among the larger on the island; however, it is still small in comparison to Bridgetown and does not offer the diversity of the capital city.

Holetown / **History**

The first settlers from overseas landed on the island of Barbados in 1627 — in the area which is now Holetown. This area was the first to be founded on the island, then under the name Jamestown. This area then lost importance to the more strategically significant city of Bridgetown.

Over the centuries, Holetown's importance was based on sugar processing. Holetown was a metropolis for those employed in this branch of the industry — and this remains so even today.

Holetown / **Sights**

Memorial: The simple name "Memorial" or "Monument" refers to the area in the centre of Holetown where the first British settlers landed. A commemorative plaque was added here on the 350th anniversary of this event.

Porters: The manor house of Porters is located on the northeastern edge of town and dates back to the 17th century. It is worth seeing for its architecture which is typical for this region and historical epoch. Large portions of this complex were first built in the 18th and 19th centuries. The house itself is not open to the public; however the gardens are accessible at varying times during the winter months. These times are available on Barbados through the Tourist Board *(→ Tourist Information)*. *St. James Church:* This Anglican church has existed in its present-day form since 1874, when the former wooden construction was replaced by stone. The wooden church was built on this site in 1660. The baptismal font and the bells both date back to the 17th century.

Holetown / **Practical Information**
Accommodation
The following is a listing of hotels and apartment complexes in the greater Holetown area, from south to north. Listings do not imply a recommendation.

Paradise Village & Beach Club (Black Rock, St. Michael — halfway between Bridgetown and Holetown), Tel: 424-0888.

Tamarind Cove Hotel, St. James, Tel: 432-1332.

Treasure Beach Hotel, St. James, Tel: 432-1346.

Smuggler's Cove Hotel, Paynes Bay, St. James, Tel: 432-1741.

Sandy Lane Hotel & Golf Club, St. James, Tel: 432-1311.

Divi St. James Beach Resort, St. James, Tel: 432-7840.

Na-Disie Apartments, Holetown, Tel: 432-0469.

Palm Beach Hotel, Holetown, Tel: 432-1384.

Discovery Bay Beach Hotel, St. James, Tel: 432-1301.

Sandpiper Inn, St. James, Tel: 422-2251.

Coral Reef Club, St. James Beach, Tel: 422-2372.

Colony Club Hotel, St. James, Tel: 422-2335.

Glitter Bay Resort, Porters, St. James, Tel: 422-4111.

Banks
Bank of Nova Scotia, Holetown, Tel: 432-1662.

Barclays Bank, Sunset Crest / St. James, Tel: 432-1472.

Canadian Imperial Bank of Commerce, Sunset Crest / St. James, Tel: 432-6760.

Royal Bank of Canada, Sunset Crest / St. James, Tel: 432-1010.

(Note: Sunset Crest is a district of Holetown with a highly developed tourist infrastructure. It is located south of Holetown adjacent to the Sandy Lane Golf Course.)

Beaches
The →*beaches* in the greater Holetown area offer excellent swimming.

Car Rental
Sunset-Crest Rent-A-Car, Suncrest, St. James, Tel: 432-1482.

Medical Care
There are numerous physicians listed in the yellow pages, the nearest larger hospital is Queen Elizabeth Hospital in Bridgetown, Tel: 436-6450.

Restaurants
The following is a list of restaurants and bars in the greater Holetown area from the south to the north, whereby only restaurants not in the hotels are listed. Other restaurants (often very good) are in the hotels themselves which are listed above under "Accommodation":

Fiesta Restaurant, Prospect-on-sea, St. James, Tel: 425-1107.

Rose & Crown Restaurant, Prospect, St. James, Tel: 425-1074.

Reid's Restaurant, Derrick, St. James, Tel: 432-7623.

La Cage aux Folles, Paynes Bay, St. James, Tel: 424-2424.

Coach House English Pub, Paynes Bay, St. James, Tel: 432-1163.

Ferns, Inn on the Beach, Holetown, Tel: 432-0385.

Barbados Pizza House, Holetown Beach, Tel: 432-0227.

The Fathoms, Benwee Paynes Bay, Tel: 432-2568.

Carambola, Moorlands Derricks, Tel: 432-0832.

Raffles, Holetown, Tel: 432-1280.

Shopping
Holetown offers very good shopping as does Sunset Crest, especially appropriate for holiday travellers. There is a variety of supermarkets as well as a Cave Shepherd department store in Sunset Crest.

Sports and Recreation
The sports and recreation especially along the western coast are plentiful — both on land and in the sea. Parasailing is offered here (Cunard Paradise Beach Hotel). Also located here is the Sandy Lane Golf Course — with 18 holes, this is the larger of the two golf courses on the island. For more information on sports and recreation as well as addresses, see under the heading →*Sports and Recreation*.

Transportation
By bus, there are excellent connections to Bridgetown and from there to all other destinations on the island. An alternative is to take the bus north to →*Speightstown* and board the "City-Bypass" bus crossing the

island to →*Bathsheba.* Holetown and Bridgetown are accessible via Highway 1, running parallel to the coastline and continuing north to Speightstown.

Important Addresses

The police station for the St. James district is housed in the historic "Plantation Fort" and can be contacted by phoning the central police telephone number 436-6600.

Holiday Apartments →*Accommodations*

Holidays and Celebrations

On official holidays, the banks and most public offices are closed. Many stores also remain closed on these days; however hotels and restaurants remain open as usual. One thing one should pay attention to are changes in the scheduled flights — but this only when the holiday is celebrated on several islands in the archipelago.

Small shops and supermarkets in the areas where hotels are concentrated (the southern coast between Bridgetown and Oistins and the western coast between Bridgetown and Holetown) often open for a few hours despite the official holiday.

Official Holidays on Barbados:

January 1 — New Year's Day

January 21 — Errol Barrow Day

Good Friday

Easter Monday

May 1

Whit Monday

First Monday in August — Kadooment Day

First Monday in October — United Nations Day

November 30 — Independence Day

Christmas Day and Boxing Day

Minor holidays include the Queen's Birthday on April 21 and the Crown Prince's Birthday on November 14.

In addition to the official holidays, there are a number of **Festivals,** which are celebrated more colourfully than the actual official holidays. On Barbados, these are:

Holetown Festival (three days in February): This festival commemorates the arrival of the first British settlers in 1627. It is celebrated around the monument in →*Holetown,* where the first settlers landed. This festival is celebrated with street markets, parades, dancing, sporting activities and games with the climax being the crowning of the Festival Queen. Oistins Fish Festival in March: This two-day festival in this, the most important fishing town on the island, includes fishing boat races, fish-cleaning competitions, exhibitions relating to the fishing industry and of course countless colourful fish, prepared and served along the streets. This festival lasts well into the wee hours of the morning with singing and dancing accompanied by the rhythms of a steel band.

Crop-Over Festival (Several weeks during mid-summer): This festival is in celebration of the sugar cane harvest, which is also used in the production of the important commodity rum. The origins of this festival

A costume parade during the Crop-Over Festival in celebration of the sugar cane harvest

can be traced well back into the history of the island; however, it was not celebrated for a period of time. It was awakened from its slumber fifteen years ago and is now celebrated to honour the efforts of the plantation workers and the men and women employed in the sugar processing industry. The Crop-Over Festival has developed into a colourful spectacle, celebrated the entire island over. Each individual community on the island sets up festival committees which are responsible for the organisation of the festival within their region. A great deal of creativity is demonstrated in this process — the only rule is that it must be fun. In most regions of the island the Crop-Over is celebrated by costume parades accompanied by music as well as a variety of cultural events. The fourth and last of the large festivals on the island is the *National Festival of Creative Arts*, which takes place in November culminating with the celebration of Independence Day on November 30. The festival includes photographic, artistic and handicrafts exhibitions. While the Crop-Over Festival is more similar to a Mardi-Gras atmosphere, the National Festival is less extravagant. Still, this festival does offer insight into the daily life, culture and mindset of the Barbadians.

The exact dates of these festivals vary from year to year, but are available from the Barbados Board of Tourism *(→Tourist Information)*.

Other Festivals: In addition to the larger festivals celebrated all across the island, there are also a number of local festivals. These are mainly religious in nature like congregational festivals, processions etc. The exact dates of these celebrations vary and are only set a few months in advance. One should inquire locally or at the Barbados Board of Tourism *(→Tourist Information)*.

Hospitals

The two large hospitals on Barbados are the public Queen Elizabeth Hospital in Bridgetown, which (when including the private stations) can accommodate around 600 patients (Tel: 436-6450) and the Catholic St. Joseph's Hospital in the St. Peter district. In addition to these, there is also a large psychiatric clinic.

The private clinics often specialise in various areas of medicine and supplement health care on the island.

→Medical Care

Identification →*Travel Documents*

Information →*Tourist Information*

Insurance

Most travel agencies offer comprehensive travel insurance which includes coverage for everything from luggage, accidents, illness and liability. This is usually a relatively inexpensive alternative, although one should compare prices since these tend to vary.
→*Health Insurance*

Jolly Roger →*Maritime Attractions*

Language

The official language on Barbados is English, which is also true for most of the surrounding islands. French is spoken on Martinique and Guadeloupe.
The accent spoken on Barbados is "bajan" and can be quite difficult to understand at times for the unaccustomed ear.
Dialects also dominate on the French Antilles, where Creole is spoken — even those who speak French will find they often still don't understand a word.

Maps and Informational Material

It is difficult to find maps with only the island of Barbados. Most are of the entire Caribbean.
Bartholomew World Travel Maps, "West Indies and the Caribbean."
Hildebrandt's Travel Map, "Caribbean."
Both of these maps can be found in most book stores.
In addition, there is a large amount of informational material on Central America on the market which does provide some information on the Antilles. These provide a good overview of the Caribbean, but an atlas is just as good for this purpose. For travelling on Barbados, such maps are virtually useless.
Many maps and informational brochures are available on Barbados itself (→*Tourist Information*).

The best map of the island of Barbados is available in the Cave Shepherd department stores free of charge (→ *Tourist Information and Shopping*). This map has a large folded format and distinguishes between the main thoroughfares and auxiliary roads with different colours. It also includes many towns and villages in the island's interior as well as banks, police stations, hospitals, restaurants and hotels. The map is supplemented by an insert maps of Bridgetown and the tourist centres along the southern coast between Bridgetown and Oistins.

Maritime Attractions

In addition to the broad range of aquatic sports and attractions on land there are also various maritime tourist attractions in Barbados.

Jolly Roger Pirate Cruises: Aboard this old pirate ship in the tradition

A replica of the "Jolly Roger" pirate ship offers visitors the opportunity to go snorkeling or to take part in the boisterous "pirate games"

of the Henry Morgan and the Sir Francis Drake, one can experience the Caribbean sea of the western coast of Barbados. One can also swim in various bays, scuba dive along the beach, go snorkelling or even take part in the "pirate games." Barbecued steak or flying fish as well as drinks (both with and without alcohol) are served non-stop. The tour lasts several hours and the price includes the taxi transfer from the hotel to the deep water harbour in Bridgetown. The price is around £22 (US$ 44). An alternative is an evening cruise with a similar programme beginning at sunset.

There are times when it can get quite crowded on board.

Jolly Roger Cruises, Bridgetown, Tel: 436-6424.

Atlantis Submarine: The Atlantis Submarine lies around a mile off the coast. Visitors are brought out to the submarine by yacht departing every hour starting at 9 am. A total of 28 passengers per trip are brought to

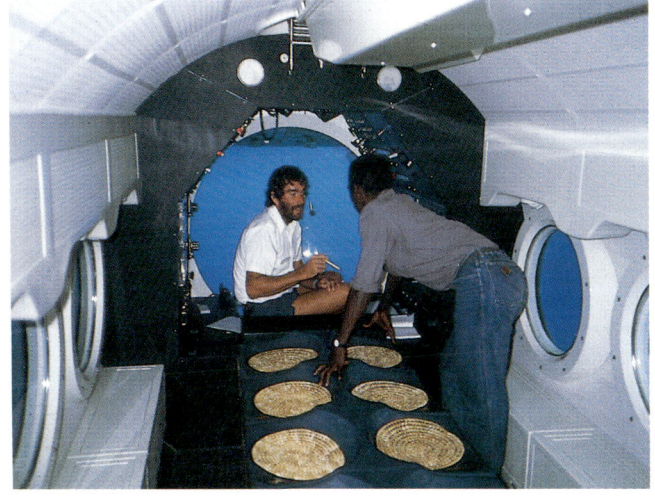

A peek into the cabin "Atlantis" submarine — one of the tourist attractions off the coast of Barbados

the submarine, which then submerges into the colourful underwater landscape of the coral reef. The submarine passes the sunken freighter "Stavronikita." Accompanying the tour musically is Bach's Brandenburg Concerto while one observes the colourful fish and coral through the large portholes. This is an especially interesting tour for those who do not scuba dive since they may have never seen these views of the underwater world.

Reservations for this tour are recommended. Atlantis Submarine, The Wharf, Bridgetown, Tel: 436-8929 (for reservations); Tel: 436-8932 (for information). The price for this tour is around £40 (US$ 80) per person; children from 4 to 12 years of age pay half of the adult price.

Bajan Queen: The Bajan Queen is a replica of a historic Mississippi Riverboat. It is more spacious than the Jolly Roger and has ample seating and tables. Other than these differences, the programme offered is quite similar. The tour lasts around four hours and the price includes a dinner buffet and drinks. The price for this tour is about £22 (US$ 44); Tel: 436-2149 or 436-2150.

Maxwell →*Dover, Maxwell, St. Lawrence*

Medical Care

As if the British had left their calling card, many of the structures and cultural remnants are evidence of the fact that the island was a British colony up until 1966. The Barbadians ("Bajans") value organisation, sometimes have a tendency toward bureaucracy, have typically British parliamentary and educational structures — and the medical care on the island is also similar in character. Medical care is considered — not lastly due to the relative prosperity of the island and the resulting technical facilities of the hospitals — as good and reliable well beyond Barbados itself. In addition to general practitioners, there are a number of specialised medical practices. Most of these specialists studied medicine in the United States, Canada or Europe and speak excellent English without the accent or colouring prevalent among the island's residents.

The standards of medical training is generally good. In addition to two larger hospitals in Bridgetown and St. Peter, there are a number of private clinics and medical practices in various other towns.

→*Hospitals, Pharmacies, Health Insurance, Emergency, Medication*

Medication

The most important thing to remember to bring along on the trip to Barbados is sun tan lotion with a high protection factor. The rays of the sun can be merciless in this region so near to the equator — one should, therefore, only spend a short time in the sun at first and then increase exposure gradually. There is the risk of sunstroke if one is not careful. In addition, one should bring along ointment for sunburn, in case one underestimated the sun's intensity. The unaccustomed foods and climate of the island can lead to a mild case of diarrhoea, making it a good idea to bring along the appropriate medication for this such as charcoal tablets. In addition, it is important to bring along a disinfectant for minor injuries and insect bites as well as any prescription medications taken on a regular basis.

→*Equipment, Pharmacies, Medical Care*

Money

The currency of Barbados is the Barbados dollar (Bds$), which is equal to 100 cents. In circulation are coins of 1, 5, 10 and 25 cents as well as a one dollar coin; notes are in the denominations of 1, 2, 5, 10, 20 and 100 dollars.

The exchange rate for the Barbados dollar is based on the US dollar and has parallelled the significant fluctuations of the past years. The exchange rate in relation to the US dollar is stable at 2 Barbados dollars to 1 US dollar.

The black market for hard currencies is non-existent on Barbados due to the stability of the nations currency. It is best to exchange US dollars or traveller's cheques in US dollars to exchange upon arrival. A word of Barbadian bank etiquette: when in line at the bank to exchange money, one should definitely wait behind the red line.

There is also a currency exchange office in the Grantley Adams Airport. Its business hours are based on the arrival of international flights.

The leading bank in the Caribbean is Barclays Bank, operating a number of branches on Barbados. The banks are open from 9 am to 3 pm from Monday to Thursday and 9 am to 1 pm on Fridays.

One can also exchange money in most hotels, although the exchange rates are somewhat less favourable.

In many stores, it is possible to pay in US dollars, especially at the car rental agencies and for organised tours. Some of these only accept US dollars.

With the development of the tourist industry, the US dollar has become a second currency on the island.

Eurocheques are not accepted on Barbados; however credit cards are accepted almost everywhere.

Barbados dollars may be taken in and out of the country in unlimited amounts; however, they must be declared.

There is a problem in exchanging Barbados dollars when travelling to the French Antilles. The banks on these islands only exchange this currency into French Francs.

Morgan Lewis Windmill

The Morgan Lewis Windmill is the best preserved of its kind on the island. It is located directly below →*Cherry Tree Hill* in the St. Andrew district on the eastern coast.

Its origin dates back to the time that the Dutch imported sugar cane to British Barbados from South America for further processing. They brought along original plans from their homeland for the construction of the windmill.

One can see dilapidated windmills scattered across the island. However, what is special about the Morgan Lewis Windmill is that it was completely restored by the Barbados National Trust and can therefore give visitors an impression of sugar processing two hundred years ago.

One interesting aside is that this windmill is depicted on every coin minted on Barbados.

Directions from Bridgetown: take Highway 1 or 2 to Greenland and from there, turn north to Shorey. Continue on the rural road to the Morgan Lewis Windmill.

Depicted on every Barbadian coin: the Morgan Lewis Windmill in the northern regions of Barbados ▶

Mount Hillaby

Mount Hillaby is the highest elevation on the island, reaching an altitude of 340 metres (1,112 feet). It is located in the southern portions of →*Turner's Hall Woods,* directly on the border between the St. Andrew and St. Thomas districts halfway between the western and eastern coast. Directions from Bridgetown: take Highway 2 via Green Hill and Eden Lodge; shortly before the town of Warren, there is a fork in the highway. Turn left onto Highway 2A leading inland and passing Holetown. Shortly after the turnoff for Highway 1A, turn left onto the rural road and continue for a few miles before reaching Mount Hillaby.

Music →*Folklore*

Newspapers and Magazines

There is no problem finding British and United States newspapers on Barbados. In addition to these, the local newspapers are also readily available. The two daily papers published on Barbados are the "Barbados Advocate" and "The Nation," which focus on national and local news. These also cover international news, but in a more or less limited sense.

These newspapers offer information on the current entertainment and events. Both papers also publish visitor magazines every 14 days available free of charge at most hotels. These are the "Sun-Seeker" and "The Visitor."

Every Sunday, the "Sunday Sun" also appears on the newsstands. →*Tourist Information*

Nicholas Abbey

Nicholas Abbey was built in 1650 in the typically British architectural style and served as the residence for a plantation owner. It overlooks the →*Scotland District.* There are two aspects which make Nicholas Abbey interesting: first the architectural aspects like its fireplaces metres in height build after English, Scottish and Welsh prototypes. In the tropical heat of Barbados it can be safely assumed that these were never used. The interior is furnished with classic British furniture. Admission is presently Barbados $2. The other interesting aspect of this estate is the tropical surroundings. The lush vegetation surrounding the building is a composite of the plant life of various regions of the island. One will find extensive sugar cane fields, gnarled mahogany trees and palm trees up to 30 feet in height (around 100 feet), in the branches of which, one might be lucky enough to see some wild apes.

The gateposts are crowned with iron pineapples which emphasises the plantation character of this estate.

A barn in the courtyard of Nicholas Abbey has been transformed into a small makeshift cinema. Shown here is a black and white film about the former generations of the family who lived here, their sea passage to Barbados and sugar processing. Souvenirs like postcards and brochures on the building are sold in the main building.

The times when this building is open vary, but are usually between 9 am and 4 pm. Exact times are available through the Tourist Board (→*Tourist Information*) or in the tourist magazines.

Directions from Bridgetown: drive along the coast via →*Holetown* and →*Speightstown* on Highway 1 past Mile and a Quarter in the St. Peter district. The road is in good conditions and leads through the aromatic sugar cane fields. A few kilometres past Mile and a Quarter, the road makes a sharp curve to the right, while a rural road continues straight on. Continue on the rural road and after a few hundred yards, turn right to Nicholas Abbey.

This trip can be combined with a visit to the →*Morgan Lewis Windmill* and →*Cherry Tree Hill.*

North Point

As one might guess from the name, North Point is the northernmost point on the island, where the Atlantic waves break on the rugged coastal cliffs, mixing with the turquoise water of the Caribbean Sea. The contrast in the colour of the two bodies of water can be easily seen.

In the direct vicinity of North point is also *Animal Flower Cave,* a network of caverns accessible over a steep and often slippery stairway. Inside this cavern, consisting of several chambers are a number of sea anemones of various colours. If touched, they quickly retract their tentacles and are also often referred to as the "flowers" of the sea.

The population of sea anemones is consistently decreasing: too many tourists have decided that they would make a nice souvenir and cut them off of the rocks without thinking — meanwhile this is strictly prohibited. One must almost constantly wade through ankle-deep water to reach the most interesting parts of the cave — at times the cave is not accessible at all. To be sure, one should check with the Tourist Board for the current conditions *(→Tourist Information)*.

Above the stairway, local guides offer their services in accompanying the tourists down the stairs and showing them "the most beautiful places which no one knows." If one chooses to accept these services then the guide does expect a tip. It is best to agree on a price before beginning the tour to be on the safe side. In addition, sturdy shoes with non-slip soles are recommended for this trip at all times of the year.

North Point is accessible from Bridgetown by taking Highway 1 via Holetown and Speightstown and continuing on Highway 1B. Shortly before Dene Hollow, turn onto Highway 1C and near Nessfield onto the rural road. Follow this road until shortly before the town of Content. Take the second right (also a rural road) toward the town of Roaches and continue on foot to the nearby North Point (St. Lucy district).

Nudism

Swimming or sunbathing nude is not permitted on the island of Barbados. The local residents are deeply religious and are even quite offended by topless bathing. There are no official or unofficial nudist beaches. Those who hope to find some secluded bay will also be disappointed because no bay is secluded enough that one does not run the risk that someone might wander by. Thus, it is best to wear a bathing suit and respect one's host *(→Conduct)*.

Those who by all means hope to be able to swim nude in the Caribbean should choose the French Antilles where nudism is possible on specified beaches, and is more accepted by the local residents.

Oistins

The fishing town of Oistins is the westernmost of the four largest towns on Barbados. At the same time it marks the end of the hotel zone which stretches from →*Bridgetown* via →*Hastings,* Rockley, *Worthing,* St.

Lawrence, →*Dover* and Maxwell to Oistins. As all of the other towns listed above (with the exception of Bridgetown), Oistins belongs to the district of Christ Church.

Oistins / **History**

Oistins is among those towns which were founded within the first twenty-five years of British settlement. It was here in 1652 that the plantation owners who were loyal to the British crown surrendered to the troops of Oliver Cromwell in the "Ye Mermaid's Inn." They signed a document which did guarantee the conquered island certain liberties and limited autonomy (→*History*). Oistins was named after a farmer family which ruled this region for decades.

The beach of Oistins: the name of the boat is, however, not typical of the Caribbean

Oistins / **Sights**

Christ Church Parish Church: This Anglican church is situated somewhat above the actual city of Oistins, built in 1837. An older church stood on this site until it was destroyed by a hurricane shortly before the present-day church was built. However, the real claim to fame of this church is that it is allegedly haunted. There have been a number of instances which remain unexplained. Every time the Chase family tomb in the western portion of the church cemetery was opened, the coffins were arranged differently without the possibility of outside influence. It is also said that the individual members of this family were not on good terms with each other. It was only when the family members were buried in separate graves that these incidents ended. The way to the "Mystery Vault" is marked.

Fish Market: The fishing town of Oistins is — understandably enough — famous for its fish market. This takes place directly on Highway 7 on the outskirts of town in a pavilion originally built for selling fish. The fish market is especially good during the winter (mornings) — in summer, there is less activity. This is because this is also the low season for the fishing industry. Somewhat farther west (on Highway 7 heading toward Bridgetown, one can see the colourfully painted fishing boats on the white sand of the beaches. Occasionally, new fishing boats are also built here on the beach.

Oistins / **Practical Information**
Accommodation
Barbados Windsurfing Club Hotel and Golden Sands Apartment Hotel are located halfway between Oistins and Maxwell (→*Dover/Maxwell/St. Lawrence).*
Banks
Barclays Bank, Oistins, Tel: 428-7444.
Canadian Imperial Bank of Commerce, Tel: 428-6184.
Beaches
The beaches on the outskirts of town are well suited to swimming. They are also well frequented by local residents, while the beaches directly near the hotels on the southern coast are more heavily populated with tourists. The area around the harbour is less suited to swimming.

Medical Care

The Queen Elizabeth Hospital in Bridgetown is around 13 kilometres (8 miles) from Oistins (Tel: 436-6450). Physicians in Oistins: Dr. Roland Hinds, Tel: 428-6717; Dr. Roland Moseley, also Tel: 428-6717. Pharmacy: Edghill's Pharmacy Ltd., Tel: 428-9481.

Restaurants

Chefette's Restaurant Oistins, Tel: 429-2223.

China Gardens Restaurant & Bar, Maxwell Main Road, Tel: 428-8179; in addition to these, there are a number of smaller bars.

Shopping

Shopping is quite good in Oistins. At the eastern entrance to the town toward the airport is a relatively large supermarket with a wide selection and a few shops surrounding it. Smaller grocery stores can be found along Highway 7.

Transportation

There are bus connections from Oistins to Sam Lord's Castle, Bathsheba and in the opposite direction to Bridgetown from the various bus stops along Highway 7. One of these stops is right near the fish market.

Important Addresses

The police station is on the eastern outskirts of town and can be reached by phoning 436-6600.

Oughterson Wildlife Park

Oughterson Wildlife Park is an area which has for the most part been left in its original condition on the property of one of the many manors in the eastern coastal regions of the St. Philip district.

Directions from Bridgetown: take Highway 4 via Constant to Turnpike and then continue on Highway 4B passing Brighton, Frenchs and Byde Mill to Summervale. From there turn left onto the rural road to Oughterson.

Paynes Bay →*Holetown*

The People of Barbados

Barbados is home to around 280,000 people, whereby the largest proportion of the population is concentrated in the southern portions of the island. A total of 120,000 people live in Bridgetown alone, with the population of the city increasing. When considering the islands area *(→Geography)*, Barbados counts as one of the five most densely populated countries in the world.

In the heavily populated southern regions, town seem to lap over into the next without any distinct city limits or they are within the metropolitan area of Bridgetown. The only thing left of old and historical towns of Hastings and Dover are the names. Despite the population density, the typical, colourfully painted huts surrounded by well tended gardens have endured. The north, in contrast is by no means densely populated. This is also the case along the western coast beyond Oistins, but entirely untouched landscapes no longer exist.

Ninety percent of the Barbadians are black or mulatto, five percent are whites and the rest are Asian. Barbados is often sited as being exemplary

Tolerance begins in childhood: the population of Barbados is composed of several races — racial conflicts are almost non-existent

for compatibility between races because racial conflicts are apparently unknown to the island and there is no trace of racism. The original inhabitants of the Caribbean Islands were peaceful Arawaks, who were displaced by "Carib-Indians" immigrating from South America. These peoples were consequently wiped out themselves just as quickly and mercilessly by the Spanish and Portuguese conquerors.

The largest proportion of the population is composed of descendants of blacks who were abducted and sold in the new world as slaves. The people's open and friendly character is widely praised — the Barbadians are considered to be very hospitable, charming and spirited as well as being polite.

First and foremost, the tourist must learn to smile back just as heartily as one is greeted *(→Greetings)*. One can definitely learn what it truly is to smile on Barbados.

Young ladies in school uniforms: the strong British influence on Barbados cannot be overlooked

In addition, "stress" is foreign to the island — it would conflict with the "Caribbean way of life" which is based on the principle of "if I don't get it done today, then I'll do it tomorrow — maybe." Fittingly, punctuality is not a strength of the Barbadians, maybe because no one is annoyed if someone shows up late. With the constant temperature of 25 °C (77 °F) and a high level of humidity, life seems to be paced more leisurely — everything seems to happen more slowly; those who have a more agitated pace will definitely succumb to the heat.

The colourful lifestyle of the local residents begins at nightfall (when the temperatures drop slightly) and continues far into the wee hours of the morning. The setting is usually one of the small bars which line the streets outside of the hotel districts. The lively atmosphere is augmented by the fact that the residents of the Caribbean are avid dancers and musicians.

At least once a year, the Barbadians overcome the heat and set their spirit loose during the day, This at the "Crop-Over" festival during the height of summer (→*Holidays and Celebrations*).

Barbados has a sensationally low level of illiteracy of less than five percent, and also the best educational system in the Caribbean. It is set up strictly according the British prototype which is not only reflected by the school uniforms. The general level of education is high and Barbadians read a great deal. Newspapers are widely read and there is a distinct level of political interest.

There are the rich and the poor on Barbados as well, however the distinction between these classes is less crass than is the case elsewhere. On Barbados, one will not find magnificent mansions next to ramshackle huts and there are no slums as can be found in the larger cities of South and Latin America.

Pharmacies

In larger cities and towns, there are pharmacies which meet the standards of most western industrial countries. The products are usually produced in the United States or England, so there should be little problem finding medications. However, if medications are taken on a regular basis, it is best to take an ample supply of these along as well as the

informational slip of paper included in the packaging. If the medication cannot be found, then an appropriate substitute can be identified.
→*Medical Care, Medication, individual entries*

Photography

Whether professional or amateur: Barbados is a paradise for photographers with its fascinating motifs, uncommon for anywhere else but the Caribbean. One problem is photographing people who do not like having their picture taken without first being asked. Even if one does ask the reply is a clear no, which one should respect. Even when taking a picture of a group of people it can happen that many will turn away and other will react annoyed. Therefore an important recommendation: never forget to ask — even if the rate of success might be very low. Sometimes a tip is expected — for others, merely offering money is an insult. Therefore, one must be extremely diplomatic when taking pictures of people in the Caribbean.

One can have more luck when photographing children, but they too expect to be asked before the shutter is snapped. Especially children are happy with a friendly thank you and a small (really small) tip.

The light conditions on Barbados are best for photos during the morning and late afternoon hours. The sunlight during the midday is often too bright and a UV filter will be necessary.

Film can be found without any problems on Barbados — unless the film needed is not the common 35mm as is the cast with professional films, disc film etc. Prices are higher than on the North American continent and Europe. The film is usually fresh in the shops; however, the high humidity can cause problems with the film. For these reasons, it is recommended to bring ample film along. Batteries are also readily available unless one requires special types of batteries.

A protective bag for sensitive film can be of use. On Barbados the security equipment at the airport is "film safe" but this may not be the case on the neighbouring islands. Film should be packed in the carry on since luggage checked is subject to a stronger x-ray.

The best way to protect film from the heat and humidity is to store the film in the refrigerator in one's hotel room or apartment.

Developing film on the island is very expensive. Therefore, it is better to wait until returning home.

Police

The harbour police can be recognised by their traditional uniforms with white shirts, dark blue trousers, blue and white scarves and light coloured hats with the broad brim. As is the case with all police officers on Barbados, they carry no weapons. The other officers have simpler uniforms but can easily be identified as police officers.

The police department is also responsible for issuing valid drivers licences for Barbados. The police can be reached by dialling 112 in an emergency; otherwise, by phoning the central police switchboard 436-6600.

Police stations are located in Bridgetown (Central Police Station, Coleridge Street), Worthing / St. Lawrence, west of Hastings, at the airport in Christ Church, in Summervale / St. Philip, Knights / St. John, Castle Grant / St. Joseph, near Belleplaine / St. Andrew, between Content and Crabhill / St. Lucy, in Speightstown / St. Peter and in Holetown / St. James. In addition to the central police station, there are two other police stations in St. Michael to the north of the city on Highways 2 and 3.

Politics

Barbados is considered the most politically stable state in the Caribbean. The form of government is democracy after the British model. The British Queen Elizabeth II is the head of state. She is represented on Barbados by a governor-general.

Today, there are two main adversaries for the political power on Barbados — both are social democratic parties. Elections take place every five years. The parliament was formed in 1639, making it the third oldest in the British Commonwealth — the 350th anniversary was celebrated quite lavishly and — as is usually the case in the Caribbean — colourfully and festively as well. The high point was a visit from the Queen in March of that year.

Earl of Carlisle had extensive privileges in the early years of the British settlement of Barbados. He could determine the borders on the island as long as there was a consensus among the local land owners. The Earl delegated this power to a governor appointed by him who stood in counsel with the council. Members of the council were in turn appointed by the governor. Two captains grappled for the title of governor after the death of the Earl, whereby one was to win the advantage through a trick. He presented an alleged document from the king which appeared to award him authority. Thus, he won the respect and support of the land owners on the island. This governor was able to maintain office for one full year. During this short phase, the parliament was founded in 1639 — a council of 34 representatives. Directly following this development, a delegate from the king informed the governor that he was to be replaced by his adversary — the parliament, however, remained intact. As is the case with the British model, Barbados has a two-chamber parliament. Growing out of the original Legislative Council was the upper house or senate with its 15 members nominated by the governor and confirmed by the British monarch. Today, the upper house consists of 21 senators who are appointed by the governor-general — twelve of these are nominated by the prime minister, two by the oppositional leader and seven by the governor-general himself. The lower house was predominantly a forum for the plantation owners at the beginning of the parliament's development. Today, a representative is elected in each of 27 voting districts on the island. Although the right to vote was dependent on one's level of income in earlier days, this has been changed. As of 1950 all Barbadians who are 21 years of age were eligible to vote. Meanwhile the voting age has been lowered to 18, as is the case in many other countries. During the 1986 elections, the Democratic Labour Party won 24 of the 27 seats in the lower house.

Porters →*Holetown*

Postal System

The main post office — formerly in the Public Buildings directly on Trafalgar Square in Bridgetown — is now in its new building on Cheapside Road in Bridgetown.

The post office is open Monday to Friday from 7:30 am to 5 pm.

Each district on the island — a total of eleven — has at least one post office of its own. The hours of operation for these is Mondays from 7:30 am to noon and from 1 to 3 pm; Tuesdays to Fridays from 8 am to noon and from 1 to 3:15 pm.

The postal system is reliable. In Bridgetown, the post is delivered twice daily and once in the more rural regions. A postcard takes around one week to reach Europe from Barbados if sent by airmail and less to reach the North American continent.

Postage stamps are available in every post office, many drug stores, souvenir and stationery shops as well as in museums and hotels. The airmail rate for an overseas postcard is around Barbados $1. The postage stamps are also very popular with stamp collectors because of their colourful and unusual motifs.

Mail boxes are painted red. It is, however, recommended to deposit letters and cards directly into the boxes in the hotels or to take them directly to the post office since the mail boxes are emptied less often in Barbados. The better hotels will have telex and telefax service available to guests for a fee.

→*Telephones*

Public Transport → *Travel in Barbados*

Radio/Television

There are three radio broadcasting stations on Barbados which can be received over the normal airwaves:

Barbados Rediffusion is a sub-company of the Nation Group which also publishes the daily newspaper "The Nation" and the weekly "Sunday Sun." Barbados Rediffusion broadcasts from Sunday to Friday from 5:30 am to shortly after 11 pm; on Saturdays from 5:30 am to shortly after midnight. The same station also broadcasts the "Voice of Barbados" a programme which can be received daily from 5:30 am to 1 am. The broadcast frequency is 750 kHz.

Barbados Broadcasting Service broadcasts at the FM frequency of 90.7 from 5:30 am to 1 am.

Caribbean Broadcasting Corporation is the state run radio and television station, headquartered in The Pine, St. Michael. *CBC Radio* broadcasts Sunday to Thursday from 5:28 am to 2 am and Friday from 5:25 am continually to 2 am Sunday morning. The frequency is FM 98.1 and AM 900 KHz. *CBC-TV* broadcasts in colour every evening from 5 until 11:30 pm on channel three.

Music is the main focus for Caribbean Broadcasting and Barbados Redif-fusion and the news also is local in character. Some of the news, however, is from the BBC World Service and/or Canadian News.

Many private homes as well as the better hotels have installed parabolic antennae making it possible to receive a number of United States television stations.

One nice way to "collect" a souvenir of Barbados is to bring a walkman with recording capability and record steel bands, the sounds of the city and radio broadcasts as one sees fit.

Ragged Point

Ragged Point is a peninsula in the extreme eastern portions of the island. A lighthouse stands here among the cliffs of the rugged Atlantic coastline, which has been a pitfall for ships over many centuries.

The construction of this lighthouse could only be begun after the death of the infamous pirate Sam Lord (→Sam Lord's Castle) since he made his fortune from luring ships into this reef and then pillaging them.

Directions from Bridgetown: take Highway 4 via Constant to Turnpike and turn onto Highway 4B following it to the end near Thicket. Continue straight onto the rural road toward Golden Grove. From there, turn left toward Marley Vale and head toward the sea as far as the road goes.

Religion

One will find a large diversity of religious confessions on the island of Barbados. However, as one would tend to expect in "little England," the largest proportion of believers are of the Anglican faith.

In total, there are more than one hundred confessions and denomina-tions on the island, including (in alphabetical order) Baptists, Christian Scientists, Church of the Nazarene, Church of God, Hindus, the Jewish faith, Catholics (Roman Catholics), Methodists, Mormons, Pentecostal, Protestants, Pilgrim Holiness, Seventh Day Adventists and a multitude of others. Also resulting from the relatively high educational standards, the voo-doo and black magic cults do not play a role worth mentioning. This is very different from the situation on the neighbouring islands where rituals are in practice which combine the voo-doo and Roman Catholic beliefs. Voo-doo is especially common on the island of Jamaica and in parts of Hispaniola; on the island of Martinique there are still "magic healers" who mix potions and are venerated as medicine men by the populace.

Barbados is characterised by a broad religious tolerance — conflicts between confessions and denominations are rare if at all existent.

Consequently, the people are deeply religious, conservative and sensitive as well — one should therefore practice consideration. For these reasons, bathing topless or nude is offensive to the local residents as is promenading through the towns in swimwear *(→Conduct)*.

As is the case everywhere, people do not take kindly to being photographed while practising their religion — be sure to respect this.

Many churches can be visited when services are not being held. For this, it is recommended to wear long trousers or skirts and to keep one's shoulders covered. Anglican church services are held five times on Sundays and once on weekdays (at 10 am) in the St. Michael Cathedral in Bridgetown. Also, there are church services taking place at varying times on Sundays in St. Paul's in Bridgetown, in St. Martin's in St. Philip, in St. Matthew's in Hastings and in St. James Parish Church in Holetown. The exact times are posted at the respective churches.

The times for Catholic mass are as follows. St. Patrick's Cathedral / Bridgetown, Sundays at 7 and 8:30 am and 6 pm; on all other days at 6:30 am and 6 pm. In addition to these, mass is also held at St. Dominic's in Maxwell / Christ Church, Our Lady of the Rosary in St. John, Our Lady of the Universe in Black Rock, Our Lady of Sorrows in St. Peter and St. Francis of Assisi in St. James.

Restaurants *→Cuisine and individual entries*

Rockley / Rockley Beach *→Hastings*

St. Lawrence *→Dover / Maxwell / St. Lawrence*

Sam Lord's Castle

Once the residence of the infamous pirate Sam Lord *(→Ragged Point)*, Sam Lord's Castle is now a luxury hotel (operated by the Marriott group) with every amenity. It is located in the eastern coastal district of St. Philip. This stately mansion with pinnacles on its roof was built in 1818 by Sam

Lord and originally furnished with works of art and English furniture.
The stucco work on the interior walls of the main house is the work of
Italian sculptors; the thickness of the walls is similar to that of a fortress.
Lord's men would hang lights in the palm trees near the beach and feign-
ed the harbour of Bridgetown to the oncoming ships. The ships would
then run aground on the reef off shore, would wreck and were plundered
by Sam Lord and his men.

Even today, the main house is still furnished as it was in the times of
the infamous pirate, whose men are said to have murdered many ships'
crews. The main hall of the house can be visited; however the rooms
can only be seen if they are vacant. The hotel also has a restaurant;
Tel: 423-7350. There is also a branch of the Bank of Nova Scotia at Sam
Lord's Castle, Tel: 423-8210.

*Sam Lord's Castle: the residence of the infamous pirate Sam Lord is
now a hotel*

Directions from Bridgetown: take Highway 6 east to the junction with Highway 5. Turn right and follow the highway till it ends at Ruby and Robinsons. From there continue straight ahead on the rural road. Keeping right, follow the signs to Sam Lord's Castle.

Scotland District

Because of its similarity to the landscapes of Scotland and its rough expanses in part, this area along the eastern coast is unofficially known as the Scotland District. This region stretches along the eastern coast including the districts of St. Peter and St. Andrew, extending to St. Joseph. Although this region has little tropical ambience to offer, it is one of the most attractive landscapes that the island has to offer. The Scotland District not only offers sugar cane fields covering the rolling hills, mahogany trees tousled by the wind and a number of other picturesque scenery, but various distinctive sights as well, like →*Cherry Tree Hill,* →*Nicholas Abbey,* →*Morgan Lewis Windmill* and →*Chalky Mount.*

Directions from Bridgetown: take Highway 1 past Speightstown, crossing the entire island heading eastward until coming to Highway 2. Continue on Highway 2 which later becomes Highway 3A and 3 through the Scotland District and leading back to Bridgetown.

Ship Travel →*Travelling to Barbados, Travelling to other Islands*

Shopping

The best shopping is, of course, in the capital city of Bridgetown, where the shops are usually tourist-oriented and for the more exclusive tastes. These types of shops are situated along the centrally located Broad Street, the "heartbeat" of the island metropolis. Local residents prefer to do their shopping in the shops and at the stands along the narrower and more quaint Swan Street. Swan Street runs parallel to Broad Street. The largest department store and least typically Caribbean in terms of its architecture is the "Cave Shepherd" on Broad Street in Bridgetown. This department store chain with its broad selection also has stores located in →*Speightstown,* north of Speightstown near →*Six Men's Bay,* on the southern edge of →*Holetown,* in →*Hastings / Southern Coast* as well as operating a duty free shop in the →*airport*. It is of course more convenient to shop in one of these department stores, but it is more interesting to venture into the smaller shops, which are more reminiscent of the colonial times. In these shops, one can chat over the prices with the salesclerk or try to bargain with the prices.

In general, the articles on Barbados are expensive, especially considering that the island is not self-sufficient and must import a great deal of its supplies. Naturally, this has an inflationary effect on the prices. It is, however, interesting to have a look at the selection offered or merely window shop, noting the origin country of individual articles: matches from Trinidad, pineapple jam from Guyana and so on. The individual countries in this region of the Caribbean trade heavily with one another levelling out the deficits.

Especially reasonable in price are the fresh fruits which one simply *must* try because the aroma is fantastic and cannot even compare to the tropical fruits available at home. The most common fruits on the islands are: mangoes, pineapple, grapefruit, bananas, guavas and carombole (a type of gooseberry which grows on trees. It is used mainly for decoration, but is also made into jam. They are shaped like a cucumber). In addition to these, there is a broad selection of vegetables like breadfruit, yams, eggplant, okra, squashes and banana figs.

Also of interest are the fresh fish, the colours of which range from metallic blue to bright pink and yellow. These are not only pretty in appearance, but also reasonably priced. The best place to purchase fish is the fish market in →*Oistins*, taking place every morning. The fish speciality of the island is the "flying fish" which can also be see on the logo for the Barbados Board of Tourism. Because of its odd appearance, this fish makes a popular (and delicious) souvenir. Those who plan on taking one of these fish home, should best purchase one in the duty free area of the airport directly before departure. In the airport, there is a small but obvious shop which has specialised in selling this fish.

As is the case anywhere, one should pay special attention to the expiration dates on food products. There are still occasional problems with the supply of dairy products, simply because the island has no dairy cows. In order to combat this problem, a large number of dairy cows has recently been imported from Canada. All in all, grocery shopping

Barbados is expensive. The cost of living on the island is relatively high — and this even includes the cola prices in the supermarkets.

Such supermarkets are especially prevalent near the apart-hotels on the southern coast. These are situated directly along Highway 7 or on the St. Lawrence Coast Road. The supermarkets are open Monday to Friday from 8 am to 4 pm, Saturdays from 8 am to noon. Smaller shops do not adhere exactly to these times — at some times they are open even longer and at others they are unexpectedly closed. The shops in the tourist areas are often open for a few hours on Sundays.

Another Tip: the fruit juices in the half-litre cans are a special treat. These can be enjoyed in the concentrated form (which is especially aromatic) or they can also be diluted with tap water. A reminder: don't forget that a can opener may not be available in the hotel room and should be brought along.

One article which is inexpensive everywhere is the island speciality "Barbados Rum" — also the export hit. For the 170 millilitre bottle, on will pay around £1 ($2) — the larger the bottle, the better the price in relation to the volume. However, one should note the customs regulations upon returning home.

Typical for the Caribbean and relatively inexpensive are the extremely colourful trousers and t-shirts as well as the ever-popular Hawaiian shirts, which are a fashion basic among the tourists as well as the local residents.

Barbados is also widely known for its naive paintings. Although the local masters are virtually unknown in other countries, their works sell quite well on the island — mostly to tourists, whereby the price is negotiable. However, Barbados does not lead in this area. Jamaica is considered the "artist's island" of the Caribbean. Among the handicrafts available on Barbados are wooden carvings, in which the African origins of most of the Barbadians can be noted.

A good place to find handicrafts in Bridgetown is "Pelican Village," a handicrafts centre on Princess Alice Highway (Tel: 426-1966). Articles offered here include baskets, wickerwork, coral jewellry, carvings and paintings.

Sitting along the roadsides are sometimes women selling hand-made dolls with hand-sewn clothing. The prices are negotiable but are around

£7 ($14), which can certainly be considered reasonable considering the amount of work which goes into producing these.
(→*Bargaining*).

Occasionally, one can purchase crystal, watches, perfumes and photographic equipment less expensively than at home; however, one should have a good idea of the relevant prices in order to have a comparison.

Other typical souvenirs are records or cassettes with the rhythms of this region — samba, calypso, reggae — as well as postage stamps (in the Caribbean, these are generally very colourful with interesting motifs; on the neighbouring islands, many series have portraits of Disney characters which have become an export commodity). Another typically Caribbean item is the coral jewellry, mostly necklaces.

Many hotel boutiques are well stocked and also have such souvenir articles. However, one must note the fact that the prices here are notably higher than in the department stores and shops in Bridgetown. Those who have ample time should definitely compare prices.

Generally speaking, the selection of products available on Barbados is quite comprehensive. There are neither empty store shelves nor are there lines in front of the shops. That which is not available in this, the "El Dorado" of the Caribbean, is much harder to come by on the neighbouring islands — the exception to this rule being the French Antilles Martinique and Guadeloupe.

In conclusion, the peddlers remain to be mentioned, who can be seen virtually everywhere along the streets near the hotels. Among their selection is a wide range of junk but also weavings, mats and hats
(→*Beaches*).

Duty-Free Shopping: Those who plan on shopping duty free should make mention of this at the cash register when paying. Name, departure date, airline and flight number are taken down and the articles purchased are transported to the airport where they can be claimed upon departure by presenting the receipt. This is, however, only possible if the articles are purchased at least 24 hours in advance of departure. Delivery to the hotel or even to one's home abroad is also often possible.

The shops in which this type of duty-free shopping is offered are for the most part on Broad Street and Swan Street in the centre of Bridgetown. There are only few duty-free shops in the departures area of the airport. There are sometimes special regulations which apply to cruise passengers whose stay on Barbados is less than 24 hours. Information on these regulations is available through the Board of Tourism (→*Tourist Information*), from the travel organiser or directly at the Customs Office at the deep-water harbour northwest of Bridgetown, where the cruise ships dock.

In stores, there are two different prices: "take-away" and "in-bond." The first are for articles which are taken along immediately without taking advantage of the duty-free tax savings. "In-bond" prices apply to those who shop duty-free.

Six Men's Bay

A whaling fleet was stationed in the small town of Six Men's Bay north of Speightstown for a number of years. Today, some ruins are still visible evidence of these activities — among other objects are some old canons which were set up to protect the whaling fleet from attacks. Directions from Bridgetown: take Highway 1 via Holetown to Speightstown. From there, turn onto Highway 1B and continue straight ahead for a short distance (St. Peter district).

Speed Limits

Within city limits, meaning almost the entire southern coast, the speed limit is 20 miles per hour and 30 miles per hour outside city limits. When considering the density of the population, these speed limits are certainly justified — one should not succumb to the temptation of driving faster even if others do so.

Speightstown

Speightstown is the northernmost of the larger metropolitan areas on Barbados and is considered the second largest city on the island. It is, however, not of such importance — touristically speaking — as is for example the more southern city of Holetown. There is nowhere near the conglomeration of hotels and restaurants in and around Speightstown with its many old wooden houses as there is in Holetown.

Speightstown / **History**

This city has its name from the British merchant family Speight, who organised the overseas transport of sugar from the harbour. There was regular ship traffic to Bristol, so that Speightstown became the counterpart of this port city leading to the epithet for Speightstown of "little Bristol." The Speight family still plays a decisive role in the British city of Bristol. With the end of the sugar boom, Speightstown seems to have missed the boat somewhat in terms of development — making the profile of this city all the more interesting.

Speightstown / **Sights**

There are no marked individual sights in Speightstown, but the city as a whole is very interesting since numerous one and two-storey wooden houses have been preserved, many over one hundred years. The architecture of these houses is typical for Caribbean port cities.

Speightstown / **Practical Information**
Accommodation
Eastry House Hotel, St. Peter, Tel: 422-2201.
Sandridge Beach Hotel, St. Peter, Tel: 422-2361.
Cobblers Cove Hotel (with a restaurant), St. Peter, Tel: 422-2291.
Heywoods Resort, St. Peter, Tel: 422-4900.
Banks
Barbados National Bank, Speightstown Branch, Tel: 422-4104.
Barclays Bank, Speightstown, Tel: 422-2194.
Canadian Imperial Bank of Commerce, Speightstown Branch, Tel: 422-2429.
Royal Bank of Canada, Speightstown, Tel: 422-2352.
Medical Care
There are a number of physicians in Speightstown; the nearest larger clinic is Queen Elizabeth Hospital in Bridgetown. Pharmacies are located in the centre of town; however, Holetown does have a larger selection.
Shopping
The selection in the shops is centred on the demand of the local residents — still there are also smaller supermarkets where those preparing their own meals can find everything they need. The department store chain

Cave Shepherd has a store in Speightstown and on the way from Speightstown to →*Six Men's Bay*.

Sports and Recreation

There are a number of places one can swim along the broad beaches in the greater Speightstown area. The hotels offer a wide range of recreational activities.

Transportation

The "City Bypass" to and from Bathsheba crosses the entire island. There are frequent bus connections to Bridgetown and a taxi stand in the centre of town.

Important Addresses

The police station is located somewhat outside of town (to the northeast) and can be contacted by calling the central police number 436-6600.

Sports and Recreation

The range of sports and recreational activities on Barbados could hardly be more diverse. The quality of this selection is due to two factors: first, tourism brought not only interest for such facilities but the financial motivation to develop them. Secondly, The Barbadians are fans of sports and recreation themselves. Even before the development of tourism, the island had very good sports and recreational facilities.

Participation Sports
Tennis

An increasing number of hotels have their own tennis courts. If more than one is present, then at least one of them will usually be lighted. Use of the tennis courts is free of charge for hotel guests or for a small fee; whereas non-guests can only use the courts for a higher fee, and then only if no hotel guests are interested in using them.

The Hilton Hotel, the Sandy Lane and Sam Lord's Castle also have their own tennis instructors.

The tennis courts of the University of the West Indies (Cave Hill, Tel: 425-1310) and Marine House (Tel: 427-5420) are free of charged for local residents and their guests.

Storm clouds gather signalling a tropical rain shower — Caribbean impressions ▶

The following clubs have tennis courts:

Paradise Beach Racquet Club, Tel: 424-0888.

Paragon Tennis Club, Dalkeith Ridge Britons Hill, Tel: 427-2054.

Rockley Country Club, Rockley / Christ Church, Tel: 427-4438.

Golf

There are two golf courses on the island, suited to different levels of ability. The most difficult of the two is the Sandy Lane (Sandy Lane Golf Club, Sandy Lane, St. James, Tel: 432-1493, -1145, -2019). This 18-hole course south of Holetown is directly near the Sandy Lane Hotel and is laid out as two nine-hole courses which can be played together or separately. The club also has a driving range and practice greens, a golf shop, golf carts and caddies. The prices for nine holes are between £8.50 and £13.50 (US$ 17 and US$ 27) and for eighteen holes, between £10 and £15 (US$ 20 and US$ 30) depending on the season. Equipment can also be rented.

The smaller 9-hole golf course at the Rockley Country Club in Rockley / Christ Church (Tel: 427-4438) charges around £3 (US$ 6) less than Sandy Lane.

Horseback Riding

A number of riding stalls offer excursions on horseback with experienced guides, including rides along the beach. When making reservations one should consider one's own ability and ask for an appropriate horse.

For one hour, prices range from £10 to £12 (US$ 20 to US$ 24) depending on the season. The price often includes the transfer from and back to the hotel.

Brighton Riding Stables, Tel: 425-9381.

Caribbean International Riding Centre, Sion Hill House, Christ Church, Tel: 423-0186.

Wilcox Riding Stables, Wilcox Hill, Christ Church, Tel: 428-3610.

Windsurfing

The larger hotels have facilities for various water sports which they offer their guests either free of charge or for a small fee. Rental surfboards are most easily found along the southern and western coasts. One will pay from £5 to £7 (US$ 10 to US$ 14) per hour or £13 to £17 (US$ 26 to US$ 34) per day.

The calmer western coast is more suited to beginners; more advanced surfers can try the southern coast. The rough seas of the eastern coast should only be attempted by experts who are also well acquainted with the island — the currents here are dangerous. It is predominantly the local residents who surf here (→*Beaches*).

"Mistral" operates windsurfing clubs in Maxwell (Tel: 428-9095) and Silver Sands.

Scuba Diving

There are a number of underwater destinations for scuba divers with interesting shipwrecks and coral reefs on the western and southern coasts. There are also a number of diving schools and diving excursions are also offered. Information on the schools and the diving tour organisers is available from the Tourist Board (→ *Tourist Information*) or at the hotel reception. Larger hotels frequently offer their own diving programmes.

The "Dive Boat Safari" is especially well equipped (including a decompression chamber) Hilton International Barbados, Needham's Point, Tel: 427-4350 or 426-0200; with daily tours to the reefs and shipwrecks, night tours, snorkelling, a diving school and rental equipment.

Prices are around £20 (US$ 40) for one dive and around £70 (US$ 140) for six dives (including equipment and decompression).

Waterski and Jetski

There are a large number of companies on the south and west coasts offering a wide variety of aquatic sports. Listed here are only a few of these:

Blue Reef Watersports, Miramar Hotel, St. James, Tel: 422-3133.

Jet-Ski Rentals, Holetown, St. James, Tel: 432-1340.

Sandy Beach, Worthing, Christ Church, Tel: 428-8000.

Willie's Water Sports, Paradise Beach Hotel Water Sports, Tel: 425-1060.

The prices are around £9 (US$ 18) for 15 minutes of waterskiing and £9 to £10 (US$ 18 to US$ 20) to rent a jetski for 15 minutes.

Deep-Sea Fishing and Yachting

The waters surrounding Barbados are very rich in fish. One reason for this is the island's geographic location farther east of the Antilles arch (→*Geography*). Charter boats cost from £120 to £150 (US$ 240 to US$ 300) for a half day and six persons. Some of the waterskiing and jetski agencies also rent out charter boats (For example, Paradise Beach Hotel Water Sports). In addition to these are the following:

Jolly Roger Ltd., Deep Water Harbour, Bridgetown, Tel: 436-6424.

Tiami, Tel: 425-5800.
Bajan Queen, Tel: 436-2149.
Sin Bad Sailing Cruises, Tel: 425-9346.
Irish Mist, Tel: 436-9201.

Parasailing
The prices vary drastically for parasailing; an approximate price range is from £10 to £17 (US$ 20 to US$ 34) for fifteen minutes. One agency which offers parasailing is Paradise Pirate Water Sports in Paradise Village & Beach Club, Black Rock / St. Michael, Tel: 424-5299.

Spectator Sports
Basketball and Cricket
Cricket is the national sport of Barbados, but both basketball and cricket games can often be seen. Dates and times can be found in the local newspapers or are available through the Tourist Board in Bridgetown (→*Tourist Information*).

Polo
Polo is another popular sport on Barbados. As with basketball and cricket, the dates and times can be found in the local newspaper or are available from the Tourist Board.

Marathon
Every year at the beginning of December, the Barbados Marathon takes place. International runners participate in this event. The exact dates are available from the Tourist Board and their international offices (→*Tourist Information*)

Horse Racing
Horse races take place five times a year (in February, around Easter, and in May, August and November) at the Garrison Savannah in the southeastern districts of Bridgetown directly near the Barbados Museum. It also seems that the islanders have adopted the British affinity for betting: even horse races in Europe are shown in the betting offices in Bridgetown — and live if possible.

The decorative tower near the Garrison Savannah where horse races are held regularly ▶

St. John's Church

From the cliffs high above the eastern coast in the district of St. John, there is a magnificent panorama of the entire coastline past →*Bathsheba* and all the way to the →*Scotland District*. St. John's Church stands here, exposed to the wind and weather, and is considered the most English of all churches on Barbados because of its architectural style. The church was built in 1836.

Behind the church is an old cemetery in which Ferdinando Paleologus is buried. According to his claims, he was a descendent of Emperor Constantine.

Directions from Bridgetown: take Highway 3 until it branches into Highway 3B at Market Hill and continue until the highway ends. This will lead directly to St. John's Church.

Telephones

Those who enjoy talking on the phone for lengthier periods of time will be glad to hear that all telephone calls within Barbados are free of charge. However, there are charges for calls to other islands. Each minute to the nearest island of St. Lucia costs around £50p (US$1). There is a minimum length for calls to Europe of three minutes and this is charged whether the time is fully used or not. One should count on paying around £10 ($15) for the first three minutes and each additional minute costs around £2.65 ($5.35). International calls from hotel rooms are often much more expensive since the hotels add a surcharge to the calls per minute. It is possible to dial direct to the United States and Europe from most public phones. The international access code is 011. This is followed by the area code for Great Britain, the country code 44 followed by the city code omitting the initial zero.

The international code for a call to Barbados from Great Britain is 010 1 809. From the US, simply dial 1-809 followed by the number.

Theft

The risk of theft on Barbados is no higher than elsewhere, but it is considerably lower than in parts of South and Latin America. Due to the relatively high level of prosperity and the high standards of education on the island, theft and crime generally remain within limits.

Still, it is of course not a good idea to stroll thorough lonesome streets and gloomy districts of town with valuable jewellry, expensive photographic equipment or large amounts of cash in one's wallet or handbag.

Visible evidence of the relatively low levels of crime on the island is the fact that the police force on Barbados is unarmed.

Time of Day

The time of day in Barbados is four hours earlier than Greenwich Mean Time (London) and one hour (New York) to four hours (Los Angeles) earlier than on the continental United States.

Tipping

As is the case anywhere, tipping is a matter of discretion and one should not feel obliged to do so. If the service was excellent, or extra effort is shown, then a tip is by all means in order.

It is customary on Barbados to round up to the nearest dollar in a restaurant or taxi, for example.

Those who want to leave a tip in excess of this should orient themselves on the 10% rule of thumb. Excess tipping can even be seen as being ostentatious.

Added to the bill in any given restaurant are 5% state tax and 10% for the service (→*Cuisine*). Still, the waiter or waitress will be pleased with a gratuity in excess of this.

As is the case everywhere where tourism plays a decisive role, wages are by no means high and tips are usually calculated into this. Tips are therefore part of the sustenance for the lower income brackets. Especially the cleaning personnel will be pleased with a tip for their service or even candy from overseas.

The residents of Barbados have their pride and if they refuse a tip, then one should not be insistent.

Tourism

"Tourism is our business — let's play our part." This slogan on the billboards spanning the street plea for support and understanding when it comes to making the tourists stay as pleasant as possible. And this, obviously with success: on Barbados, one does not encounter resentment toward tourists or tourism. Hotel complexes are by no means guarded holiday ghettos, where one does not dare venture out past dark. The Caribbean is also called "the Mediterranean of America" because during the winter months many US Americans and Canadians spend their holidays here — making the winter months the high season. However, differences do remain in comparison with the Mediterranean. One will not find high-rises, towering hotels or concrete hotel bunkers on Barbados. A hotel with more than three stories is an exception. The island must not be ashamed of any architectural eyesores originating from the infancy of the island's tourism simply because there are none. Tourism has also stimulated investment in the island's infrastructure. The best example of this is the Grantley Adams International Airport which was brought to its present condition with investments in the millions of dollars. This airport is considered the Caribbean hub for international air traffic and therefore for all tourism in this region as well. This makes Barbados the gateway to the Caribbean for those arriving from the opposite shores of the Atlantic.

The number of beds on the island, counting hotel, apartment complex and cottage capacity is around 14,000. Most of these are concentrated in the hotels in the middle to luxury classes.

In 1990, Barbados hosted 700,000 visitors from abroad, most of them from North America. However, the number of European visitors is on the rise, with marked increases in the neighbourhood of 30%.

Today, tourism on the island has become an important economic factor *(→Economy)* and provides many of the residents with jobs — although poorly paid in part. Considering the increasing population on this already densely populated island, Barbados is investing in tourism as a means of income and foreign currencies.

Tourist Information

The following offices run by the Barbados Board of Tourism offer informational brochures with general information, tips on restaurants etc. These materials are available free of charge. Also available from the Board of Tourism is a current list of the travel organisers who offer package tours to Barbados (including addresses).

Barbados
Barbados Board of Tourism
P.O. Box 242 Harbour Road
Bridgetown, Barbados, W.I.
Tel: (809) 427-2623; 427-2624
Telex: WB 2420
Fax: (809) 426-4080
There is also a branch office in the airport building.

Canada
Barbados Board of Tourism
Suite 1508, Box 11
20 Queen Street West
Toronto, Ontario M5H 3R3
Tel: (416) 979-2137
Toll-free: 1-800-268-9122
Telex: 021-06-218247
Fax: (416) 979-8726

United Kingdom
Barbados Board of Tourism
263 Tottenham Court Road
London W1P 9AA
England
Tel: 071-636-9448/9
Telex: 051-262081
Fax: 071-637-1496

United States
Barbados Board of Tourism
800 Second Avenue
New York, New York 10017
Tel: (212) 986-6516
Toll-free: 1-800-221-9831
Telex: 023-666-387+
Fax: (212) 573-9850

Barbados Board of Tourism
3440 Wilshire Boulevard, Suite 1215
Los Angeles, California 90010
Tel: (213) 380-2198
Toll-free: 1-800-221-9831
Fax: (213) 384-2763

The best source of information for the current daily events are the visitors' magazines which are available free of charge in the hotels. These provide information on everything from music festivals to folklore evenings, theatre programmes and excursions offered.

"Sun-Seeker" is the events magazine of the "Barbados Advocate," the largest daily newspaper on the island. This magazine includes, in addition to scheduled events, dates and times, a map of the island, a map of Bridgetown and a number of advertisements of restaurants and tour agencies. The "Sun-Seeker" ("your guide to fun in the sun") appears every 14 days.

"The Visitor," is also free of charged and is similar to the "Sun-Seeker." It is published by the publisher of the daily newspaper "Nation" and the "Sunday Sun." This publication also appears every 14 days.

"What's on" is the third tourist magazine. It also appears every 14 days and is available free of charge.

Finally, there is also a telephone service with information on the calendar of events, Tel: 424-0909.

In the larger hotels, there are brochures which offer information on various excursions and the island's attractions. Very good maps are available free of charge in the main Cave Shepherd department store on Broad Street in Bridgetown. These include a map of Bridgetown and a map indicating the locations of the hotels in the southern portions of the island.

→*Maps*

Tourist Season

Barbados is presently developing into a travel destination during the entire year when considering the moderate and stable →*climate*. During the winter, the North Americans visit the island, while it is mainly

Europeans who visit Barbados during the summer. High season is during the winter from November until March. Prices are highest during this time.

Traffic Regulations

British visitors will have no problems adapting to the traffic on Barbados. This is somewhat more difficult for those visiting from North America because in Barbados, one must drive on the left-hand side of the road.

Drivers not used to this should be extremely careful when turning corners as to not end up on the right (but wrong) side of the road.

The network of roadways is well maintained even though streets in the small towns tend to be narrow. Routes are well marked; traffic lights are relatively rare.

In addition to the normal city streets and rural roads is a highway network across the island. Most of the highways radiate from the capital city of Bridgetown. A new highway which is not yet noted on all maps spans the island laterally, connecting the airport with the western coast. Travel time is reduced by 30 minutes if this route is taken, making it unnecessary to drive along the southern coast.

Maps are available in the tourist information offices on the island (Harbour Road in Bridgetown and directly at the airport in the Christ Church district) as well as at many service stations.

The driving style of the Barbadians is much more spirited than most are accustomed to, but this is relatively "harmless" when compared to the driving on some of the neighbouring islands. Still, as a pedestrian, one should definitely practice caution. This is especially true for those not used to traffic on the left-hand side of the road when crossing street. One must first look to the right.

→*Speed Limits, Travel in Barbados*

Trains

With the industrialisation period in distant Europe, the British colonists began with an ambitious as well as seemingly superfluous endeavour: the construction of a railway on the island of Barbados. In 1881, the first train ran on this railway and 1938 would see the last train on the island.

Rail travel was stopped on the island because it was "too slow and too expensive," as it was stated at that time.

What is left of this era are some remnants of the rails along the eastern coast near Bathsheba — today, this is a destination for hikers which smacks of the romantic days of yore, offering a somewhat morbid atmosphere with the rusting rails under the tropical undergrowth and palm trees. This area can be reached via Highway 3 from Bridgetown to Bathsheba and continuing north along the coast.

→*Travel in Barbados*

Travel Budget

As mentioned briefly in other sections of this book *(→Shopping),* the cost of living on Barbados is relatively high. Therefore, one should plan

The network of roadways on the island of Barbados is in good condition; within the cities, the streets can be quite narrow

enough into one's travel budget to cover these costs. Accommodation in standard rooms in a middle class hotel will cost around £25 (US$ 50) for a single and £35 (US$ 70) for a double during the summer. During the winter months, these prices are approximately double. The price for one night in a single room of the Hilton Hotel — not even among the most expensive on the island — is between £58 (US$ 116) and £113 (US$ 226) during the summer. The Barbados Board of Tourism *(→Tourist Information)* publishes a list of accommodation prices every six months, which are available free of charge.

One can save money by booking a package tour from one's home country, usually including the flight, accommodation, breakfast, transfers and the local travel director. The tour organisers purchase their quotas in blocks and are therefore able to offer substantial discounts on the normal prices.

"Island hopping" is a relatively inexpensive way to see a number of islands in the Caribbean

Price information for grocery shopping and restaurants is included under the heading →*Cuisine*.

Taxi prices are high, whereas the buses are inexpensive and operate to all regions of the island (→*Travel in Barbados*).

One must plan at least £100 (US$ 200) per person into one's travel budget if one plans on visiting one or more of the neighbouring islands. This price does not include any flights. Those looking for an inexpensive option for a family holiday will find Barbados to be a less suited alternative.

Travel Documents

Entering Barbados is not complicated. Still, one is confronted with the friendly but thorough officials at the large and well laid out Grantley Adams International Airport. Sometimes this thoroughness does lead to a bureaucratic endeavour.

Those who do not plan on staying on the island longer than three months do not need a visa, whether visiting from the United States or from an EC member state. What is required is a valid passport. The passport should be valid for at least six months after departure. In addition to the passport, one must fill out an immigration card. Note that the immigration officials check these meticulously and will ask about anything which is unclear before stamping it. Therefore, one should take care in filling out this document. Immigration cards are provided on board the airplane before landing.

Upon entering Barbados, one must also present one's ticket for the return flight — this is just as important than having a passport. If one does not (yet) have a ticket for the return flight then entry is usually strictly denied. What is then possible is to proceed to the ticket counter accompanied by a customs officer and to purchase a return ticket. Quite often, it is also necessary to disclose one's financial situation to prove that expenses incurred while staying on the island can be covered. Once this procedure is complete, it varies as to how many times the passport is stamped: usually it is once, sometimes it is twice — this, however makes no difference as to the validity of the entry documentation.

Even if there are a large number of people waiting at the passport control, it is definitely recommended to wait behind the red line on the floor until the official signals the next in line to proceed. This is also the system used in many banks and post offices.

If staying on Barbados for longer than three months, it is required to apply for a visa. Information on this process is available from the →*Tourist Information* offices. Another option is to extend one's stay at the Immigration and Passport Department, Careenage House, The Wharf, Bridgetown; Tel: (809) 426-9912.

Other than this, there is the option to leave Barbados near the expiration of one's three months, visit a neighbouring island and reenter. This automatically entitles one to stay an additional three months. However, do not forget a return ticket when reentering Barbados.

Those who want to become permanent residents of Barbados must contact the Immigration and Passport Department (address listed above). It is, however, recommended to first contact the Honorary Consulate in one's home country.

Upon departure from Barbados, an airport tax of Barbados $ 20 is levied. The tax stamp for this is affixed to one's ticket when checking in. This must also be paid when checking in so that one has proof of having paid this tax when continuing to the passport control.

Bringing along pets to Barbados is very complicated. Because the island has no rabies and the fact that the government would like to preserve this situation, pets must be quarantined in Great Britain for six months. Only after this process can one apply at the Ministry of Agriculture, Food and consumer Affairs. Graeme Hall, Christ Church for permission to bring along one's pet. The port of entry for the pet must also be approved by this ministry.

In order to be able to drive on Barbados, a national or international driving licence must be presented at one of the police stations in Hastings, Worthing or Holetown. It is, however, best to take care of this directly at the airport. This costs Barbados $ 10. The international driving licence is not valid without having gone through this process. The car rental agencies on Barbados will help expedite this process, which is understandable since their business depends on this.

Travel in Barbados

The transportation on Barbados is uncomplicated since no restrictions apply. There is a well structured bus system which operates to all regions of the island as well as 800 miles of roadways.

Travel in Barbados / **By Bus**

The bus system is well developed on Barbados, whereby most long-distance buses operate without a fixed schedule, but do run relatively frequently (on the southern coast, every 15 to 20 minutes, less often inland). It is almost impossible to get lost or take the wrong bus because, with the exception of the "City Bypass" bus from Oistins to Speightstown and the bus from Bathsheba to Speightstown, all buses operate to and from Bridgetown.

The bus stops are marked and those heading to Bridgetown are marked with "City." If this sign is not present, the bus runs inland (away from Bridgetown). One must remember that traffic is on the left-hand side of the road, or it can get confusing. Each bus has a sign on which the destination is written. The buses are blue and yellow and rather old and somewhat rickety, but by Caribbean standards, these are modern.

It does not suffice to merely wait at the bus stop: the bus will only stop if one waves or signals to the driver in some way. If the bus still does not stop, then this means it was full to capacity.

The bus lines are structured in such a way, that one can plan a tour of the island by bus (for example, from Bridgetown to Oistins or Bathsheba then crossing the island to Speightstown and returning to Bridgetown). The bus fare is — regardless of how long one stays aboard the bus — around 35p (75 US cents) for all routes. One must then pay again when one transfers buses. For this reason, there are no bus tickets. One may only board the bus in the front where a conductor sits with a funnel-shaped apparatus. The sum is checked through a type of peep hole and then the money falls into a sack or box. Change is never available making it highly advisable to carry an appropriate amount of change when planning on bus travel. With a little luck, one might even experience the Caribbean atmosphere on the bus itself: if someone starts singing, the entire bus will join in.

There are bus terminals at three different locations in Bridgetown:

1) Fairchild Street corner of Victoria Bridge — predominantly for buses departing to the south and east.

2) At the junction of Lower Broad Street, Cowell Street and Cumberland Street — mainly for buses heading north and west.

3) On the Princess Alice Highway near Pelican Village — also for buses heading north and west.

There has been no rail service on the island since 1938 *(→ Trains)*.

Travel in Barbados / **By Taxi**
Taxi stands can be found near the bus terminals and various other central locations in Bridgetown (for example: Trafalgar Square opposite the
Public Buildings) and at the airport. Other towns also have taxi stands.
It is best to ask at the reception of one's hotel for directions to the nearest
taxi stand because this will save money. Those who call a taxi must pay
the trip from the stand to the hotel and then back to the stand after
reaching one's destination. There is no central switchboard for the taxis.
The following is a list of selected taxi telephone numbers:
Independence Taxi Service: 426-0090.
Paramount Taxi Service: 429-3718.
Barbados Transport Co-op Society Ltd.: 428-6565.

*Plants, flowers and fruits from all parts of the world make up the diverse
flora of Barbados*

In addition to these, there are some hotels in the upper categories which offer their own taxi service.

None of the taxis are equipped with a taxometer — the prices for the most significant destinations and routes are set by the government. Still, it is best to agree on the exact price before departing to avoid unpleasant surprises. Remember that the standard prices are for the whole taxi and not per person. It is a good idea to get a copy of the taxi prices from the Tourist Board upon arrival at the airport.

The following is a list of the most important routes including approximate prices from the →*Airport:*

Hotels on the western coast — £10 to £13 (US$ 20 to US$25)

Trafalgar Square in Bridgetown — £8.50 (US$ 17)

Crane Beach — £7 (US$ 14)

Sam Lord's Castle — around £7 (US$ 14)

Oistins — £5 (US$ 10)

Speightstown — £15 (US$ 30)

Bathsheba — £12 (US$ 23)

Hotels on the southern coast — around £8.50 (US$ 17).

The way to get a taxi at the airport is that one must first go to the taxi stand supervisor. One states his or her destination and is given a slip of paper with the exact price on it. Only after this does one go to the individual taxis.

An alternative to this are the collective taxis which can be stopped anywhere along the route by waving one's hand. This, if there is still room in the taxi. The passengers pay a proportion of the cost — the set price is divided among the passengers.

Travel in Barbados / By Car →*Car Rental, Traffic Regulations*

Travel in Barbados / **On Foot and Hitchhiking**

It is definitely worthwhile to do a lot of walking around Barbados, gaining interesting insights into the daily life and culture of the island. However, one should be cautious because of the traffic and often lacking sidewalks.

Hitchhiking is not officially prohibited but the risks involved are the same as elsewhere in the world.

Travelling to Barbados

The large majority of holiday travellers in Barbados travel to the island by air — and this usually within the scope of a package tour offered by a number of travel organisations and agencies.

As a general rule, such travel packages are usually far less expensive than individually organised travel.

Travel packages are available for under £700 ($1350) including trans-Atlantic flight; prices from the United States are less expensive, depending on the departure city. Prices also depend on the type of accommodation and the number and types of excursion one plans to undertake while in the Caribbean.

Travelling to Barbados / **By Air**

There are direct connections to Barbados from London and most major North American airports. The airlines which serve Barbados are (among others) American Airlines, British Airways, British West Indian Airways, Canadian Holidays and Lufthansa. Some airlines offer a "holiday fare" where restrictions apply (minimum stay 14 days; maximum stay three months). Prices are often the same for other destinations in the Caribbean (Santa Lucia, for example) making it possible to book directly through to another island and arranging a stop-over on Barbados at no extra charge. The flight to Trinidad via Barbados is only slightly higher.

Inter-Caribbean air travel is offered through the Liat airline (→*Travelling to other Islands),* with a connecting flight to Barbados. Special fares must usually be paid in full within 24 hours of booking, cancellations and changes in the travel itinerary are only possible before departure and then an administration fee is charged.

Older travel guides often mention Caribbean Airlines, the national airline of Barbados. This used to offer inexpensive service from London to Barbados on a regular basis; however, passenger service has meanwhile been discontinued. This airline only transports freight within the Caribbean.

Another inexpensive possibility for those coming from Europe to reach the Caribbean is by taking an Air France flight from Paris to the French Antilles (Martinique and Guadeloupe) with highly subsidised "domestic fares" since the French Antilles are not independent, but count as one of the Départements of France and therefore considered French territory. From Martinique or Guadeloupe, there are connecting flights to Barbados with Air Martinique or LIAT. Information is available by contacting Air France.

Airline Passes: BWIA and Lufthansa offer airline passes, making island hopping possible *(→ Travelling to other Islands)*.

Lufthansa: The "Caribbean Explorer" air pass is only available in Europe and must be booked in conjunction with a trans-Atlantic flight offered by Lufthansa. All flights must be booked in Europe, no changes are possible and the fare is non-refundable if cancelled. Flights to the South and North American mainland are not included. The air pass includes at least three and at most six flight coupons, each for a one-way flight with LIAT or Eastern Airlines, which usually cost around £30 ($60) from Monday to Thursday and £40 ($80) on Fridays and Saturdays for the most popular routes. After each stop-over, one must use the next coupon for the next flight.

BWIA: The "Intercaribbean Fare" pass are is only sold in Europe and the travel itinerary must be set and booked before departure. The exact dates of travel can, however, be changed for an administration fee of US$ 20. The fare cannot be refunded after beginning the trip and the pass is not valid for flights to Caracas. Passes are valid for 30 days and only on BWIA flights. They include unlimited stop-overs, but only once on each island (excluding plane transfers). The price for this pass is around US$ 350.

The duration of the flight from selected cities to Barbados are as follows:

Caracas — 2 hours, 30 minutes

London and Frankfurt — 9 hours

Miami — 3 hours, 40 minutes

New York — 4 hours, 20 minutes

Rio de Janeiro — 8 hours

San Juan, Puerto Rico — 1 hour, 30 minutes

Toronto and Montreal — 5 hours

Travelling to Barbados / **By Sea**

From Southern England there is a regular freighter connection to the Caribbean, which also docks in Barbados among other islands. The price is, however, relatively high (up to $5,885/£3,335 for a cruise lasting 4 to 6 weeks).

Barbados is also often a port of call for numerous Caribbean and South American cruises, offered from a number of cities in North America and Europe (→ *Travelling to other Islands*).

Travelling to other Islands

Travelling to other Islands / **By Air**

The most important means of transportation between the Antilles is the airplane. Because of the significance of air traffic in this region, Barbados has become a transport hub and is the first landing point for many trans-Atlantic flights. At the same time it serves as a stop-over for those who continue to South America and as well as the neighbouring islands. The leading airlines in this region are:

LIAT: a full schedule of flights including several daily flights from Barbados via St. Lucia, Martinique, Dominica and Guadeloupe to Antigua (the base for this airline). This airline has mostly propeller planes manufactured by British Aerospace and De Havilland Canada with around 42 seats and little leg room. LIAT Airlines serves the following destinations: Anguilla, Antigua, Barbuda, Barbados, the British Virgin Islands, Caracas, Dominica, the Dominican Republic, Guyana, Grenada, Guadeloupe, Martinique, Montserrat, Nevis, Puerto Rico, St. Croix, St. Eustatius, St. Kitts, St. Lucia, St. Maarten/St. Martin, St. Thomas, St. Vincent and the Grenadines (Mustique, Canouan, Union Island, Carriacou) and Trinidad and Tobago.

The LIAT office on the island on Barbados is located at: St. Michael's Plaza / St. Michael's Row in Bridgetown, Tel: 436-6224 (Reservations & Information); the airport office can be reached by phoning 428-0986. The main office is located in the V.C. International Airport, P.O. Box 819 on the island of Antigua, Tel: (809) 462-0700, Fax: (809) 462-3038, Telex; 2124 AK. The prices for LIAT flights are listed in US $ and are somewhat below the international averages. The "Excursion Tickets" are especially worth recommending. These are valid for 17 days and include the return flight. The prices is only a few dollars more than a one-way ticket. These excursion tickets allow for a one stopover for each way.

LIAT has also recently begun offering "Explorer" and "Super Explorer" tickets for visitors from Europe. With these types of tickets, Barbados can be combined with a number of other Caribbean Islands. Further information is available by contacting LIAT. The "Explorer" ticket is valid for 21 days and allows for up to three stopovers. Depending on the season, the airfare is between £100 and £135 ($200 and $270). The "Super Explorer" ticket allows for an unlimited amount of stops while exploring the Caribbean and is valid for 30 days, priced at £235 ($470). The following terms and conditions apply to both of these fares: all flights must be booked and confirmed before arrival in the Caribbean; the fares are only valid in connection with a trans-Atlantic flight; no flights can be changed after the ticket is issued; only one stop-over per island is allowed, however one can use the same island to change planes any number of times. While the "Super Explorer" ticket is available throughout the entire year, the "Explorer" ticket is restricted depending on the season. During the high season (winter) it is only offered at specific times. Further information is available at travel agencies when booking the trans-Atlantic flight. It is best to book LIAT flights when booking the trans-Atlantic flights to avoid possible difficulties later.

Package tours *(→ Travelling to Barbados)* which include a tour of the neighbouring island, lunch and an English-speaking tour guide are often only slightly more expensive than the flight alone. Considering this, it might be better to consider a package tour — comparing prices is important. One agency offering such tours is, for example, Caribbean Safari Tours Ltd., Beckwith Mall, Bridgetown (Tel: 427-5100). Day trips to Martinique or St. Lucia cost around $200 as do trips between Grenadine and Barbados combining sailing and air travel.

Flying stand-by with LIAT is not at all recommended since the flights are regularly overbooked. Many passengers will find themselves waiting for the next flight even if their ticket has been checked and their boarding pass issued. For this reason, it is necessary to arrive at the airport at least 60 to 90 minutes early, check all baggage and go directly to the boarding gate. Even doing so, there is still no guarantee until the plane is moving.

In addition to this, one should reconfirm all LIAT flights at least 72 hours prior, to ensure that one is not deleted from the passenger list. There is a list of all of the LIAT offices and the destinations served in the onboard LIAT magazine ("liat islander").

When calculating the duration of individual trips, it is important to note that most flights make a number of stop-overs — four times from Barbados to Antigua — which can certainly cause delays.

BWIA (British West India Airways International Trinidad & Tobago): Those who have booked a package tour to Barbados will usually fly via St. Lucia-Hewanorra. The airplane then continues to Port-of-Spain, Trinidad. Those who plan on only stopping in Barbados and not on spending a lengthier amount of time should definitely book the flight to Trinidad before arriving in the Caribbean. The flight to St. Lucia is about the same as that to Barbados.

The following routes are served by the BWIA airline: Baltimore, Boston, Frankfurt, Cologne/Bonn, London, New York, Stockholm, Toronto; in the Caribbean: Antigua, Barbados, Caracas/Venezuela, Curaçao, Grenada, Guyana, Haiti, Jamaica, Puerto Rico, St. Kitts, St. Lucia, St. Maarten/St. Martin, Trinidad-and-Tobago.

Most Caribbean destinations serve only as stop-overs for lengthier flights, which does not hinder passengers from booking only the continuing flights.

One should, however, note that the long distance flights can easily be delayed. Due to the size of these airplanes, the danger of overbooking is much less. The only time that getting a flight might become a problem is during high season or during Carnival celebrations on Trinidad in February.

An inexpensive offer for travel between islands is the "BWIA Intercaribbean Fare" (→*Travelling to Barbados*).

In addition to the above mentioned airlines, the following also serve Barbados:

- Air Jamaica (to Jamaica)
- Cubana (to Cuba with connecting flights departing from Havana)
- Eastern Airlines (serving all of the islands)
- Guyana Airways (to Guyana)
- Viasa (to Caracas)
- Tropic Air (offering only charter flights — also can be grouped for a small group as an "air-taxi"; address on Barbados: New Terminal Building, Grantley-Adams-Airport, Christ Church, Tel: 428-0927).

In general, it is important to know that there are two airports on the island of St. Lucia, located about one hour by taxi from one another. One should allow for this if connecting flights depart from the other of the two airports. Vigie is the regional airport served by LIAT in the northern regions of the island directly near the capital city of Castries. Hewanorra to the south is the airport which can accommodate jets, serving as the destination for trans-Atlantic flights or those from the United States and Canada.

Travelling to other Islands / **By Ship**

In the Caribbean, numerous *cruise ships* circulate in the waters of the Caribbean. These offer every amenity imaginable, dock at a number of islands in the Caribbean and offer their passengers organised tours and activities on the islands themselves. These cruise ships dock in the Deep Water Harbour northwest of Bridgetown near the Princess Alice Highway. The clientele is composed mainly of North Americans; three to seven day cruises departing from Miami have grown in popularity. Some cruise lines offering cruises to the Caribbean are: P and O Lines (Los Angeles, San Juan and Puerto Rico); from San Juan: Princess Cruises, Oceanic Sun Line, Costa Line, Cunard, Chandris Line, Royal Caribbean Cruise, Norwegian Cruise Line and Carnival Cruises; from Miami: Royal Caribbean Cruises and Holland American Cruises.

Freight Ships: There is also the possibility of travelling to other islands with freighters, but this can be complicated if booking after arrival in the Caribbean. The best tip is to check with the various captains in the Deep Water harbour, at the Bridgetown shipyards. It is also true that many captains are not allowed to take passengers on board. If a willing captain can be found, the price is dependent on one's bargaining skills.

Sailing Tours: These are offered between the islands, usually combined with a flight to the Grenadines / Tobago Cays. These can be booked through agencies specialising in these types of tours on Barbados. One agency offering one and two day tours is Caribbean Safari Tours, Beckwith Mall, Bridgetown, Tel: 427-5100.

In the city harbour of Careenage / Bridgetown, there are sometimes catamarans and one and two-mast sailing vessels (for example, the "Vanessa Ann") which offer tours between the islands, stopping at Barbados. One can ask at the harbour if there is any space free and what it costs. The tourist information office *(→ Tourist Information)* can also be of help in establishing contacts.

Important: To re-enter Barbados, one must present a valid return ticket as well as a passport. Therefore, take these documents along on sailing tours or any other trip to another island.

Turner's Hall Woods

Turner's Hall Woods in the heart of the St. Andrew district is one of the last continually wooded regions on Barbados which has retained its original jungle character. Wild apes live amid the lush vegetation including white cedars, gigantic ferns etc., as is also the case with the →*Barbados Wildlife Reserve,* →*Farley Hill National Park* and the area around →*Nicholas Abbey.*

Directions from Bridgetown: take Highway 2 crossing the island past the turn off to Highway 3A, continuing on Highway 2. Shortly beyond Haggatts, turn left onto the rural road leading to Turner's Hall via St. Simons and Cheltenham.

Vaccinations

No vaccinations are required for entering Barbados. As recently as three years ago, however, Barbados did require, for example, proof of the smallpox vaccination from those who travelled in infected areas within two weeks of entering Barbados. Meanwhile, the world health organisation has declared smallpox no longer a threat, although there are isolated incidents reported in various regions of the world. This shows that vaccination requirements can change quickly or become obsolete. Although there are no vaccinations required at the moment, one should be prepared to provide proof of various vaccinations if travelling through an infected areas.

For those who plan on visiting the more forested neighbouring islands (for example Dominica), a malaria prophylactic treatment is recommended. However, for Barbados this is not necessary.

Generally speaking, however, it is advisable to have sufficient vaccination protection when travelling to the tropics. This includes polio, tetanus, hepatitis B, typhoid, cholera and yellow fever. General information on these vaccinations is available through doctors and other medical institutions.

If Barbados is the first station on a longer trip to South or Central America, then there are a number of vaccination requirements for various countries. Contact the appropriate embassies, consulates or tourist information offices for exact information.

Many travel agencies also have information on vaccination requirements on file.

Vegetation

"Isla de los Barbados" — the island is said to be named after a type of tree: when the Portuguese seafarers stopped at the island long before the British were to settle it, they called the island "Island of Beards" because of the fig trees with their beard-like foliage which lined the coast. Even today, this first impression still exists upon arrival on Barbados. With the arrival of the first settlers on Barbados in 1625, the found the island heavily wooded. Within only half a century, these woods fell victim to the axe and saw, leaving only remnants of the forests which once covered the island. Much of the wood was used in the construction of ships and houses, and the fields which remained were used in the cultivation of sugar cane. Remaining of the original forests on Barbados is only the tiny, pristine →*Turner's Hall Woods* in St. Andrew. There, one will still find the "bully trees," carob and fig trees.

During the course of the centuries, plants from all over the world were imported and planted on Barbados. These are plants which are quite frequent but not endemic to the island: tree ferns from Australia, almond trees from Africa and Asia, flamboyants from Madagascar, and jasmine bushes from Central America. Also among the plant life on Barbados is the mahogany tree which can be most frequently found in the →*Scotland District,* around →*Nicholas Abbey* in the St. Peter District and around →*Cherry Tree Hill.* These are now used only rarely in the construction of fishing boats in Speightstown.

At first glance, Barbados makes a less "tropical" impression in regard to its vegetation than is the case with St. Lucia, the Dominica and Martinique for instance. This may be due to the fact that there is no more tropical rain forest on the island of Barbados.

One word of caution in regard to some of the trees along the beach, the fruits of which are poisonous (they resemble green crab-apples).

One should not spread one's beach towel in these areas nor should one seek shelter under these trees during rain.

Also widespread are the coconut palms; an impressive boulevard lined with these trees can be found at the entrance to →*Codrington College*. Tropical fruits grown on Barbados include mangoes, limes, various citrus fruits, pomegranates, papayas, figs and bananas. Even the breadfruit (with a circumference of over 12 inches, spherical and scaly) is widespread. This fruit is originally from the Pacific region and now counts among the food staples.

The most impressive time to view the blossoming plant life on Barbados is during the off-season from April until September. The magnificent and widespread bougainvillea blooms during the entire year.

Many of the well-off islanders are great lovers of plants and have arduously tended gardens with meticulously manicured lawns. One can admire these gardens (99% of which are fenced in) from the streets during a stroll through the towns (for example, from Oistins heading north). The botanical gardens on Barbados are Andromeda Gardens and →*Welchman Hall Gully*.

Villa Nova

Villa Nova in the St. John district was once the elegant residence of a plantation owner. This two-storey house with an attractive veranda was built in 1834, having been commissioned by a certain Edmond Haynes. Portions of the valuable furnishings from the colonial period as well as the interior of this villa can be viewed on weekdays. The times when this residence with its manicured gardens can be visited do, however, vary. One should contact the Tourist Board for information on the exact times before heading out (→*Tourist Information*).

Directions from Bridgetown: take Highway 3 to Market Hall. At this point there is a trident shaped branching formed by Highway 3, a rural road and Highway 3B — continue on the rural road in the middle via Golden Ridge, Redland and Claybury which leads directly to Villa Nova.

Visas →*Travel Documents*

Water Supply

The supply of drinking water is dependable on Barbados, mainly because the storage capacity is sufficient to bridge dry periods. The tap water is of drinking quality. The water itself is filtered naturally by the coral and limestone layers of the island, stored in natural underground reservoirs. After extraction from the water table, the water requires only minimal chemical treatment.

Weather →*Climate*

Weights and Measures

Although the metric system is winning ground in the Caribbean, weights and measures are still given in the British system. Temperatures are in degrees Fahrenheit; lengths in inches, feet and yards; distances in miles; and weights in pounds.

Welchman Hall Gully

The origins of Welchman Hall Gully date back to the middle of the nineteenth century. This gully was planted with citrus and spice trees and then abandoned. What remains is a jungle like valley with a wealth of interesting vegetation. Also located here are a number of small grottoes with stalactites and stalagmites accessible over narrow pathways (St. Thomas district).

Directions from Bridgetown: take Highway 2 heading east, which leads directly by Welchman Hall Gully, shortly beyond →*Harrison's Cave.*

Worthing

This small town on the southern coast of Barbados is almost a part of →*Bridgetown* as is the case with →*Hastings,* Rockley, →*Dover, Maxwell* and *St. Lawrence.* Today, Worthing is known as a beach resort town.

Worthing / **Practical Information**
Accommodation
Cacrabank Beach Apartments, Tel: 435-8057.
Sandy Beach, Tel: 435-8000.
Sichris Hotel, Tel: 435-7930.

Worthing Court Apartment Hotel, Tel: 435-7910.

Banks

Bank of Nova Scotia, Worthing, Tel: 435-7953.

Canadian Imperial Bank of Commerce, Worthing Branch, Tel: 435-7991

Car Rental

Sunny Isle Motors Ltd., Dayton Worthing, Tel: 435-7979.

Medical Care

There are a few medical practices in Worthing and the Queen Elizabeth Hospital in Bridgetown is only a short drive away.

Pharmacy: Cave's Pharmacy, Worthing Plaza, Tel: 428-8234.

Restaurant

Rosebud Restaurant, Tel: 435-7377.

Shopping

Various shops offer everyday articles; there are also small supermarkets in town. Further stores can be found in the nearby town of Hastings.

Sports and Recreation

The same is true for this area of the island as is the case on the southern coastline: the beaches are narrower than those of the western coast and are sometimes interspersed with coastal cliffs. Still, they are composed of fine grained sand and are quite clean. The sports and recreation facilities are quite good. For further information →*Sports and Recreation*.

Transportation

There are frequent bus connections to Bridgetown and in the opposite direction along the southern coast to Oistins. Bus stops are located directly on the coastal Highway 7.

Youth Hostels →*Accommodation*

Hayit's Practical Travel

The convenient, compact companion

Reliable, condensed, current — containing the most significant information in a handy format. Practical Travel offers the alternatives to the masses, the overpriced and the tacky — avoiding the tourist traps along the way.

The alphabetical entries offer practical information without omitting the interesting, the surprising and the fascination of the local flair — the right tips to paint the setting for an unforgettable holiday.

* Aquitaine (France)
* Barbados
* California (USA)
* Dominican Republic
* Eastern Canada
* Florida (USA)
* Goa (India)
* Gran Canaria (Spain)
* Ibiza (Spain)
* Kenia

* Kuba
* Lanzarote
* Madeira (Portugal)
* Malta and Gozo
* New Zealand
* Portugal
* Provence (France)
* Tenerife (Spain)

The Hayit Edge:
* easy reference
* handy format

* practical information
* reasonably priced

Additional titleds in production   Check your local bookseller

Hayit Publishing

Hayit's Phrase Books
Keeping you in touch

Speechless? Not with Hayit phrase books, whether at the airport, in the hotel or a restaurant. The phonetic entries guarantee immediate and effortless pronunciation. A travel glossary offers ready reference — just the word you need at your fingertips.

* French
* German
* Spanish
* Italian

Additional titles in production...

The Hayit Edge:
* no previous knowledge necessary
* quick reference
* current usage with modern terminology
* concise presentation of grammar

Check your local bookseller

Hayit Publishing

Hayit's Budget Travel
The age of affordability

Keeping an eye on travel practicalities, Hayit's Budget Travel Series combines background information with in-depth coverage of regions and cities including invaluable advice on how to stretch those travel funds.

Not only as an aid in travel preparations, but a constant companion, these guides can be easily tucked into any backpack or carry-on... for those who travel off the beaten track.

* Baltic States
* Turkey
* Venezuela
* Thailand

The Hayit Edge:
* affordable approach
* comprehensive information
* ongoing revision
* practical format and content
* inside pointers...
    ...from authors who know

Check your local bookseller

Hayit Publishing